"With significant detail, Craig Gross takes the reader on a journey toward knowing the true ministry of Jesus Christ. *The Gutter* will make you rethink your values. Gross's poignant honesty and hope-filled stories will inspire you to move out of your comfort zone and help you see where it is God needs you invested."
—**Matthew Paul Turner,** author of *The Coffeehouse Gospel: Sharing Your Faith In Everyday Conversation* (Relevant Books)

"This lost world needs more people like Craig Gross, a person who is willing to live boldly for Christ. In his book, *The Gutter,* he challenges Christians to follow Christ into the dangerous places of this dark world. It is there that the light of Christ is desperately needed. I highly recommend not only reading this eye-opening book, but also asking God to change your ministry view on what it means to truly minister like Christ."
—**Dean White**, Associate Pastor, Saddleback Church,
Lake Forest, California

"*The Gutter* is incredible! It really challenged me personally to broaden my scope of ministry and to get out in my gutter and make a difference for Christ."
—**Paul Diaz,** Student Pastor, Morning Star Church, Salem, Oregon

"*The Gutter* is a great book, and what you can expect from a person like Craig Gross. His life is and ministry is exactly what Christ would be doing today, and this book not only backs that up, but shoves the reader toward the gutter as well. My favorite part of the book is Craig's outreach to the elderly woman at the nursing home. If that doesn't push you out of your comfort zone and into the lives of lost and hurting people, nothing will. This is a must read for every pastor, youth worker, and young person who consider themselves followers of Jesus Christ. Two dirty, gutter stained thumbs up!"
**—Phil Chalmers**, President, True Lies
(TrueLies.org, TeenKillers.com)

"The gutter Craig describes is a place where us, the 'little Christs', have killed fear itself and trusted love in a way that infiltrates our very being. We become like mirrors to anyone and everyone around us. They see themselves, loved, beautiful, and powerful."
**—Dave Tosti**, PAX217, speaker

"This book rocks!" **—Rob Beckley**, frontman for the group Pillar

WITHDRAWN

"With clarity and authenticity, Craig Gross shares a message of radical grace and hope. *The Gutter* will explode your stereotypes, inspire your faith, and motivate your compassion. It will challenge you to love others where they are and, in doing so, to become more like Jesus."
—**Jud Wilhite**, Teaching Pastor, Central Christian Church, Las Vegas, Nevada and author of *Faith, Hope, and Love .... That Goes the Distance* (Baker Books)

"That's one of those powerful concepts that I think most of us Christians would know in our heads but may tend to forget in our lives. It's a nice kick in the pants. I did feel challenged to re-evaluate how I live out my life, and how I can go to the gutter." —**Jason Harwell**, singer/songwriter

"*The Gutter* is honest, confrontational in its own way, convicting, and motivating. As I read through the book in many chapters I asked myself, where is my gutter? Do I have a gutter? Why not? The motivation doesn't just come from your story it comes from the life of Christ."
—**Jake Larson**, Associate Pastor, Arcade Church, Sacramento, California

# THE GUTTER

Craig Gross

# THE GUTTER

## Craig Gross

## WHERE LIFE IS MEANT TO BE LIVED

[RELEVANTBOOKS]

Published by Relevant Books, a division of Relevant Media Group, Inc.
www.relevant-books.com
www.relevantmediagroup.com
Published in association with Yates & Yates, LLP, Attorneys and Counselors,
Orange, California

© 2005 by Craig Gross
Additional writings: Jason Harper and Adam Palmer
Editor: Adam Palmer

Design by Relevant Solutions (www.relevant-solutions.com)
Cover design by Ben Pieratt
Interior design by Jeremy Kennedy

For information or bulk orders:
RELEVANT MEDIA GROUP, INC.
100 SOUTH LAKE DESTINY DR., STE 200
ORLANDO, FL 32810
407.660.1411

International Standard Book Number: 0-9760357-0-7

05 04 03 02 01 10 9 8 7 6 5 4 3 2 1

Printed in the United States of America

**This book is dedicated to Tom Ramsay** ... thanks, Tom, for reaching into my gutter and pulling me out. My life has never been the same. You are a true inspiration and a man I desire to become more and more like.

# WHAT'S IN THE GUTTER?

# ACKNOWLEDGMENTS

Just a few words to those who have helped me on my journey into the gutter. First of all, to the late Bob Briner ... thanks for writing the amazing book, *Roaring Lambs*, which made me do what I hope many will do after reading this book. Mike Foster ... what a journey! Thanks for your friendship, willingness, and desire to join me in the gutter. My wife, Jeanette ... thanks for standing alongside me all the time. Jake Larson ... thanks for asking me the tough questions and always watching out for me. Mom and Dad ... thanks for putting up with me all of these years. Jason Harwell ... thanks for all of your work on the proposal for this book. Arcade Church and Eastside Christian Church ... thanks for giving me my start in ministry. Thanks to everyone at Fireproof Ministries and XXXchurch who has worked with me over the years. And finally, to the crew at Relevant ... thanks not only for publishing this book, but for doing what you do.

This book would not have had a life without the help, direction, and support of Jason Harper. Jason, your stories and your life encourage me to do what I do. Thanks for your time, your writing, and your desire to see this book through from start to finish. Your work on this project was so valuable, and you have taught me some new words to add to my vocabulary.

Adam Palmer ... after reading the article you wrote and published about my ministry, I was blown away. Your writing, editing, and collaboration with me on this project were definitely what I needed to get this project where it needed to be. Thanks for supporting me with your band, your magazine, and your time on this project.

# MY GUTTER

## SECTION ONE

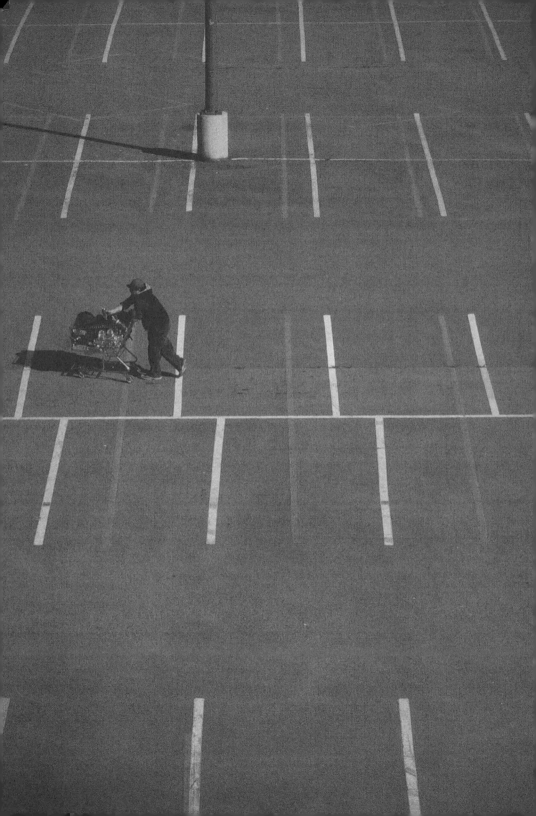

# 01
# WHAT IS THE GUTTER?
## CHAPTER ONE

It was a long time ago, but it still seems like yesterday. Maybe it remains fresh to me because it transformed my life. It was the first time I had ever been to the gutter.

A group of students and I had decided to hit the streets one cold February Saturday to hand out some sandwiches and brown-bag lunches. We headed to downtown Sacramento and quickly distributed our fifty or so lunches. With only two brown bags left, we stood at the entrance to an area known as Friendship Park.

Located across the street from a major feeding program for the homeless, Friendship Park is known for its 100-percent transient population. The park's name isn't really a good indicator of the mood inside; it's anything but friendly. And on this particular day, it was extra crowded. I looked at the students with me and decided this was where we would give out our last two lunches.

As we entered the park, I looked ahead and noticed a slightly elevated area with only three people sitting on it, self-appointed park kingpins. They glared at us, eyes screaming, "What in the world are you doing here?" Despite the visual resistance, we walked on. It felt odd, and I didn't understand why we weren't welcomed. Here we were, entering "Friendship" Park to give away some free lunches, yet we faced resistance. I did not understand the scenario; I did not understand the gutter.

We approached the trio, the apparent leader of which was a bearded man with dark, curly hair flaring from beneath a baseball hat. His eyes were hidden behind an old pair of '70s sunglasses that would be considered "retro" in another part of town. I decided to give it a shot.

"Hello, we'd like to give you lunch today," I said, my voice shaking with nervousness. He said nothing.

Little did I know how significant to me this encounter would become. I had just entered the gutter, and my heart was being changed. Growing up, I was protected from this environment; I didn't even know this other world existed. But now as a youth pastor, I not only wanted to experience it, but I also wanted others to see it too. I didn't want the kids in my group to be as sheltered as I was. In my mind, I really thought I was making a difference, but the gutter was bigger than I had expected. And more crowded.

See, I grew up in a Christian home and went to church my whole life, but that upbringing taught me about a Jesus who was with children and cute little lambs. It was a Jesus who wore a long, spotless robe, gracefully walking around with a smile on His face, speaking words of mysterious hope to the masses. This was the perception of Jesus as I grew up—a Jesus who stayed clean and vague and remote. But here on this hilltop, sandwiched between three homeless people and a group of youth who wanted to see the mysterious hope of Christ in action, I unknowingly began to discover a different Jesus. I was learning more about Him in the gutter.

Reading the Gospels now, I see a Jesus who is different from the one I knew during childhood. This Jesus is willing to take risks by loving all the outcasts—the people others avoided. He's most effectively embraced by the hurting, broken, and pretty-much-jacked-up who gather around Him. He doesn't turn them off or repel them; He draws those who have emotional, physical, or spiritual needs. The only ones who detest Jesus are the ones who believe they have it figured out, that they're immune to the streets, to the gutter. Jesus spends most of His time in with the people, not with the Pharisees. He's in the streets, not in the synagogues. He goes to the gutter.

In Luke 14:23, Jesus instructs His disciples to "go out into the highways and byways and compel them to come in." He challenged them to go to the people in need. When I became a youth pastor, I read this passage and realized there was more to it than what I'd thought growing up. It was not only an invitation into a building, a church, or a mass. It was also an invitation into a relationship with Him. It was instruction to go into the streets and establish relevant relationships.

In a new millennium, Jesus might say it this way: "Go into the gutters of the city and love people so they will love Me."

Instead of demanding that the lost come to the place where religion was being peddled, Jesus went to the gutter and found them. Then He mastered the unlikely: He learned things about them. He found things in common with them. He loved them.

CHAPTER ONE

Many times with Jesus, genuine love and hope came in the oddest of packages. It was friendship; He laughed with them. It was life; He ate with them. He healed them. He loved them. He hung out with them. He became *their* friend in *their* environment, *their* neighborhood, *their* home ... *their* gutter. He provided Hope to people with common pain and illustrated that normal people with normal problems and normal pain are the cement that forms the foundations of the gutter.

The gutter can be described in different ways with different terms. Put simply, my gutter is not necessarily your gutter. The gutter is the place where we discover that we need God most. Some would believe the gutter is attached to a lack of money. Wrong. I have seen people with millions lying facedown in the gutter. Some believe the gutter is the place with a lack of success. I have seen many gutter-dwellers who would be considered "successful" by the world's definition. Ask them and they would tell you that their success only masked the misery of the gutter. The gutter is a place believers aren't willing to go because they remember what life was like when they escaped from it.

What does the gutter look like? It's a difficult question to answer. To some, the gutter looks like Friendship Park, but to that trio on the hilltop, the gutter probably looked a lot like church. The gutter is often defined by the vantage point from which it is seen. It's a tough thing to peg, but for a moment let me lay out a workable definition of the gutter: *The gutter is the place I am least likely or inclined to go because it is a place where people are not like me; they are not Christians.*

Back to the hilltop. These thoughts were the beginning of the change in my heart, and I clearly remember thinking them as I stood before those three people in the gutter of Friendship Park. Sure, it was full of homeless people, but it wasn't defined by their lack of economic status. Instead, this gutter had many common elements: First, people, problems, and pain were presently abundant; and secondly, it was an unlikely place for the common church to look for potential new members.

4

My mind swirled, intimidated by his lack of response. I continued trying to give the trio the sandwiches as the students from our youth group looked on. "We came here today to share God's love in a practical way," I said gently. "We didn't come to preach at you, just to give you lunch." Finally, he spoke.

"We don't want your lunch! You would do yourself a favor to get on."

To the bearded man's right sat a young man, maybe twenty, silently glaring, backing up his leader's statement; on the other side was an elderly woman of about seventy-five. She was wrapped in a windbreaker jacket that advertised a local little league team, probably secured at a flea market or a clothing shelter. But what grabbed my attention were her feet. She wore no shoes, and the foggy air had caused her feet to turn a light blue, while the dirt caked around her ankles told a story of long days and longer nights on the streets. I realized she could be anyone's grandmother.

Their refusal of our lunch stunned me, leaving me discouraged by rejection. It was a pretty worthless offer, after all. My students and I hung our heads and began to retreat, and our defenseless posture must have irked the leader, because he suddenly lashed out, "How can you think your sandwich would help us? Look at her feet. Do you think your lunch can warm her feet? Can it?"

I was dismayed and at the same time innocently guilty. Our intentions were good: I mean, after all, at least we were out there. But he was right. We weren't being very wise in our gutter strategy—like I said, Friendship Park happens to be located directly across the street from a homeless-feeding ministry. Food wasn't what they needed; it wasn't the right tool to reach into this gutter. I was ashamed for not thinking this through all the way and turned around to leave. But I couldn't walk away in silence. We were there. We had set out to do something valuable and effective, and though we'd missed in our attempt, at least we had taken a swing at it.

I froze and slowly turned around. Clearing my throat of the fear that had crawled there, I said, "You need to wait a minute!" I think my sudden fiery demeanor caught them off-guard; they said nothing. "I don't know how you got here or what your story is, but we came here to help you," I said calmly. "We may not know the best way to do that, but we are here. I don't blame you for wanting a way to warm her feet, but all I have is a lunch."

And then it dawned on me. I'd said all I had was a lunch, which wasn't entirely true. Before I could move, John, one of my students, began to kneel down. I don't remember what he said, but before either of us could think about what he was doing, John took off his shoes and socks. He gently took one of the elderly woman's feet with one hand, using his other hand to set the lunch down in front of the leader, (hopefully) illustrating his heart. John wanted to meet their practical needs of hunger, yet he also wanted to do what Jesus did, in a way. He had washed feet; John wanted to warm them.

A silence settled across the park. Once John finished tying the second shoe (lightly, so it wouldn't hurt her tender feet), I looked and saw tears running down the elderly woman's face, clearing a path through the dirt that had caked on her cheeks. I gently asked what her name was.

She smiled. "My name is Billie."

"Well, Billie," I paused, holding back a complete flood of confusing emotions. "I don't think John's shoes fit too well."

The ringleader finally broke his silence. "We want to go to your church tomorrow." I couldn't hide my stunned reaction. All I could do was look at him in disbelief. "We want to go to your church tomorrow," he repeated.

It was the last thing any of us expected. I was too busy thinking about what this would look like, when John quickly said, "I'll pick all of you up tomorrow morning at 8:00 a.m." As the words came out of his mouth, I realized he was committing to something he had not contemplated. After all, we still did not know the guy's name.

"I'll pick you up here in front of the park at 8:00 a.m., but you need to tell me your name," John said.

"This is Ghost Rider," he said, pointing to the guy on his right. "And you can call me Cisco."

"Billie, Cisco, and Ghost Rider," John said, "tomorrow, we are going to church!"

## THE NEED TO GET IN THE GUTTER

My experience in Friendship Park could happen to anyone, really: anyone willing and unafraid to follow Christ into the dangerous places. These are the very same places He visited in order to reach those who were hurting and broken. Jesus Himself said the sick are the ones who need the doctor, not the healthy, and the ones who need the Ultimate Physician are often too spiritually sick to get to Him. Most of them don't even know they've been infected with the deadly disease that separates us from the Creator.

Everyone knows the gutter is where perverts and prostitutes live. It's filled with murderers and thieves, pornographers and pedophiles. But an accurate description of the gutter doesn't end there, because the gutter is a place we've *all* been, where we *all* lived before we took Jesus seriously. It may have looked different to you than it does to other people, but a gutter is a gutter, no matter why you're there.

It's no secret that our world is spinning out of control. We're constantly bombarded with news about pain, murder, rape, war, crimes, financial disaster ... the list goes on. But these stories all share the same root cause: people, problems, and pain. This is the gutter. Hurting and broken people surround us on every turn, but these people, regardless of their situation, are the very ones for whom God created a solution.

Jesus was sent to this earth *through* the gutter, to become a bridge of hope for those who live in the gutter. Regardless of how long they have been there or what circumstances took them there, they are still in the gutter. Jesus called them the "whosoever" in John 3:16: "For God so loved the world that he gave his one and only Son, that *whosoever* believes in him should not perish but have everlasting life." The Gospel is open to everyone, including those who live in the gutter.

Many times I have discovered that I banish people to the gutter when they don't believe like me, act like me, speak like me, or look like me, but it is in the gutter that Jesus defined His model for the most effective ministry. When I miss Jesus' example to the gutter, it's only because I have forgotten the pain I felt when I was in my own gutter. We forget the gutter is the one thing that we all have in common—it's the great equalizer. Why? Because we are people who have all experienced problems and pain only a gutter can produce. To go to the gutter is to be changed by the gutter. Those who are most opposed to the gutter are the ones who have been there the least.

Jesus spoke of the gutter in Matthew 25:45 when He said, "That which we do to the least of them, you have done unto me." The gutter is the place where *the least of them* live. For the religious, the gutter can be the place where people don't believe what we believe, or where people do dirty things. In other words, the gutter is where the *sinners* are.

When I accepted Christ as my savior, I was lifted out of the gutter, but I was not made better than those who remained. If I'm going to be honest and real with myself, I must remember that my own failures are no different than those of the worst sinners, because in God's eyes, sin is sin. In reality, I am the worst sinner I know. My expressions of love for Jesus can make me feel like I am better than those in the gutter, but I must remember that whatever I do to them, I'm doing to Him.

Got that? Good. Now let's talk about the book you hold in your hands. This is not a book meant for you just to read, put down, and think, "How nice." I'm hoping to spur you on to some action here, so as you proceed, consider the stories and examples contained in these pages with the following principles in mind:

1. **The Difference Between "Them" and You Is a Small One.**
   That small difference is your discovery of Jesus and how that discovery wound up making a huge difference in your life. Those in the gutter are in need of a Savior; you and I can be the ones who bring Him to them.

2. **The Only Mistake in The Gutter Is Not Going.**
   Okay, before you get the wrong idea—I'm not saying you should go into the gutter and start to live the lifestyle of that gutter. I'm saying that as long as you go on Christ's terms and with Christ's attitude, it's impossible to make a mistake. Look, I can be a lazy guy, and my procrastination has kept me away far too many times. It seems like I'm always finding ways to stay in the comfortable climate of Christian circles that make reaching the lost impossible, but that is in direct contrast to Jesus' ideas about Christian living. Jesus encouraged us to enlarge our circles and get in the gutter. We only screw up when we stay away.

3. **Identify a Need That Can Be Met.**
   Serving and meeting needs were the greatest ways that Jesus connected with people. We too can meet needs in the gutter, making our efforts more effective. Meeting a physical need before asserting a spiritual need is a great tool. Whether it is a pair of socks and

sneakers, a cold cup of water, five loaves of bread, or two fish, Jesus laid the plan for success in the gutter. Pastors and church leaders, Christians young and old, every person willing to get in the gutter can help fulfill their part of the Great Commission.

Consider the gutter. You may just meet Ghost Rider, Cisco, and Billie while you're there. Or me.

# 02
# MY GUTTER

CHAPTER TWO

I have a confession: while I'm a book writer, I'm not much of a book reader. An even more shocking confession: I especially don't read many of the books found in Christian bookstores these days (another subject for another book). But *Roaring Lambs* is different. If you haven't read it, you should. Authored by Bob Briner, *Roaring Lambs* is a wake-up call to Christians to take a look at our culture and find a way to make an impact. To be loving Christians who make a loud noise in our world. Lambs that roar.

Once I started reading it, I couldn't put it down; it was contagious. The deeper I got into it, the more I realized it was going to require me to take some action and do something about it—and myself. It sounds uncool to say this, but the book practically changed my life. Upon finishing it, I came to the realization that I was no roaring lamb. Sure, I'd done some cool stuff, but I had missed my true purpose.

See, I grew up in a Christian home, in the Christian ghetto, if you will. When I was in the sixth grade, my family moved to Sacramento, California. I was doing fine in my public school, but my older sister couldn't handle the junior high in our new neighborhood, so my parents decided she needed some shelter. After a thorough search, they found that shelter in Victory Christian School. Less than a week later, my sister was enrolled.

My parents originally were going to leave me in public school for a while, but then decided I needed to attend the same school as my sister, even though I wanted to stay where I was. I lost the battle and soon found myself sitting in Mrs. Ruff's sixth-grade classroom with a bunch of other kids whose parents were as scared by the gutter as mine were.

Unfortunately, this school did nothing for my faith. I got a decent education and a whole lot of bitterness toward my parents for sending me there. (In fact, as a result of my experience at Victory, I questioned each and every decision they made about me from then on out.) Even though it seemed like forever, I graduated from Victory Christian High School in 1993, delighted to be out.

Don't get me wrong—I am not against all Christian schools. I think there are some good ones out there. What I am *really* against is the frightened policy of Christians who separate themselves from the rest of the world. My parents sent me to Victory so I wouldn't be exposed to the "things of the world," but I just didn't get it: What in the world were they so scared of? Why did they have to be so protective? Wasn't the God living in me greater than the ones living in the world?

I think about the story in the Gospel of Luke when Jesus was twelve years old. Check out Luke 2:41-49, and you'll see a picture of Jesus at about the same age I was when I entered Victory. He and his family had gone to Jerusalem to celebrate Passover, and when the family took off for home, they accidentally left Jesus behind.

But check out what Jesus was doing while they were freaking out, scared—He was in the temple courts, or as the NIV translates, he says, "Didn't you know I had to be in my Father's house?" I like the good old King James Version even better, where Jesus says, "I must be about my Father's business."

I didn't know it at the time I went into Victory, but just like Jesus, I had to be about my Heavenly Father's business, too—and frankly, now I know that business has nothing to do with separating myself from the big scary "world." If Christians would stop being scared of the world—or the gutter—I think most of them would find out for themselves that it is definitely not the place they want to be. It's a change in perception I wish more people would adopt: to focus more on the great life we have in Christ than on the fleeting lures of the gutter. The more afraid we are of the gutter, the larger it looms and the more tempting it becomes. If we can alter our perspective to focus on Jesus, we will learn how to be about our Father's business, reaching those who are living a gutter lifestyle.

Now let's back up to the beginning of my junior year in high school. I'd been a part of the Christian ghetto for five years at this point, but even though I was submerged in all things Christian, I wanted no part of my parents' religion or my teachers' faith. It wasn't until my youth pastor, Tom Ramsay, reached out to me in the midst of my gutter and began to mentor and disciple me in the last two years of my high school career that I made the decision to give God my entire life in service to Him.

See, even though Christians surrounded me, it had no effect on me because none of them reached into my gutter and showed me an active, Christlike love. They were all words and no action. They modeled the clean, vague, remote Jesus of my youth, not the Jesus I discovered later on. It wasn't until Tom started working with me that my eyes were opened to the gutter I was living in and the life I could have been leading.

You may find it strange to think I could remain in the gutter while surrounded by a Christian environment, but it happened. (Now the opposite is true for me—I'm continually surrounded by a gutter environment, and yet I remain a Christian.) When I became a junior, Tom asked to start meeting with me weekly, and like I said, it was through those meetings that I came to really understand what following Christ was all about. Two years later when I graduated, I didn't have a clue what to do with my life, so the only thing that sounded good was to become like Tom Ramsay.

(By the way, Tom never apologized to me for confiscating my Van Halen *OU812* tape when I was in the seventh grade. He claims he still has it, and deep down I believe it's because he secretly liked it. I'm on to you, Tom.)

Freshly graduated, I headed off to another ghetto—Hope International University, where I studied to become a youth pastor. Again, there are tons of great Christian colleges, and I think I got a fine education while I was there. I learned some great things I'm still using to this day, but when I really looked at my Christian college, I found it was just an extension of Victory. It was still a safe, world-free environment, and it simultaneously outraged me and broke my heart. There was so much potential there, but it all stayed bottled up on campus and rarely spilled out into the world.

Nevertheless, I did the assignments, passed the tests, fulfilled the internships, and graduated three years later in 1996. After some job-hunting, I was eventually given the opportunity to take over the junior high department at Eastside Christian Church in Fullerton, California. It was everything I wanted, and I was having a blast.

I said earlier that I was in the gutter, and it's interesting to note that many people who get saved leave their old lifestyles and gutters and head out in a new direction to "do something for the Lord." But then there are a lot of people like me—people who head back to their old gutters hoping to reach their peers and other people there. My gutter was smack in a Christian environment, so I became a youth pastor and worked with a lot of Christian kids like me—kids whose faith needed developing and testing.

I was enjoying this ministry and found myself in a great position to stay for some time at this church, but God had other plans and shook my world up in a pretty crazy way. He called me to start an organization called Fireproof Ministries with my best friend from my youth group days, Jake Larson, a recent college graduate like me. Fireproof's mission became twofold: to win people to the Lord while training and developing people to meet the unmet needs of the world through culturally relevant ideas and programs. We wound up doing a number of things at Fireproof, mainly centered on youth and young adults. However, something always seemed to be missing.

Sure, through our programs and speaking engagements I was helping people come to know Christ and escape from their gutters, but along the way I lost my desire to get back in to the gutter. My life consisted of speaking and planning events for other people—but I never came into the picture. All my friends were Christians, all my contact was with churches and people of faith, and except for a short-term missions trip here and there, I no longer reached into the gutter on my own.

Flash forward to P.F. Chang's China Bistro, one of the greatest places on earth. It's pan-Asian cuisine at its finest, and my friend Mike Foster and I decided to go there on a whim, just to spend part of that warm June 2001 afternoon sucking up fried rice and Chang's Spicy Chicken. A week earlier, we'd been on a plane. We were flying to a youth conference in Oregon where I was scheduled to speak and Mike's worship band, the Pulse Praise Band, was going to play. It was a standard Fireproof event, until I loaned Mike my copy of—you guessed it—*Roaring Lambs* on the plane.

That's why we decided to meet at Chang's—to discuss the book and its impact on our lives and way of thinking. Once we were there, Mike started the ball rolling by dropping one word: porn.

Yes, Mike felt God had spoken just the single word to him. *That* word. That single, dirty, ugly, yucky, filthy word that we just don't talk about in church. Being somewhat of a rebel who bucks tradition (how'd you guess?), I immediately loved it. But what were we supposed to do with it? We began to brainstorm ideas, and decided right then and there to start a website. Just to get the people in the gutter interested (and the modern-day Pharisees in the Church riled), we decided to call it XXXchurch.com. We even came up with our tagline—"The #1 Christian Porn Site"—right there on the spot.

When I really want to do something, I'm the kind of guy who will just go do it. I distinctly remember that nervous race back to my office so I could register the domain name, hoping no one had it, and fortunately no one did. It wasn't long before we made T-shirts and stickers. We had no clue what we were doing, other than we wanted to help guys who like to look at naked women and don't want to talk about it. We hadn't studied the issue; we had never severely struggled with it personally. We just both liked the idea because nobody was addressing it in a relevant way. It was such a dirty little secret.

So on January 9, 2002, XXXchurch.com made its Internet debut, and, boy, were we totally *not* prepared for the response. It was a hit almost immediately, and suddenly we had all this exposure. But there's something I didn't mention—the reason for that date. See, January 9 was the opening day of the AVN Adult Expo in Las Vegas, Nevada, the largest pornography trade show in the United States.

We took our message straight to the gutter.

And they loved us.

See, we didn't know what the porn industry in general would think of us, because they're constantly under attack, and not just by religious groups. Nobody really likes them, and there are obvious reasons for that. But we decided early on not to fight that particular battle; instead we went in with a completely different approach—we went to their turf on their terms. We did what we thought Jesus would do—we went to the sinners. (Check out Luke 5:30-32 if you don't believe me.) Because we took the first step, the people in the industry got to know us. Once they got to know us, we started hearing them say, "You guys aren't like the other religious people; you aren't what we thought of as Christians."

How can this be? It's simple—we're honest about our profession, about our faith, and about our humanness. The gutter—and not just the porn industry, but the gutter at large, the real world—has embraced us, and they'll embrace the Christian message, too. They just don't tend to embrace "the Church," because they're looking for people who are willing to be real with them, not preach to them. Not that everyone gives us big high-fives every time they see us, but on the whole, we've encountered astonishingly little resistance from the industry because deep down, they're all just sinners, desperately looking for someone to love them. And that's what we do.

Since we started XXXchurch, we've had a ton of opportunities to get in the gutter, and we always bring honesty with us. Both Christians and non-Christians struggle with the issue of pornography, so we take the real-life approach, step back from all that's been said about it, and come at it straightforwardly, honestly, and controversially.

We've encountered our fair share of controversy since we started our little "church," mostly from the Christian community. We've placed our own billboard in the middle of a bunch of porn billboards, we've bought airtime on Howard Stern and *The Man Show* to air our commercials, and we've been to more porn trade shows, always bringing the same message of Christ, forgiveness, and freedom from addiction. We also bring our wives. (We aren't the smartest people in the world, but we aren't idiots, either.) We bring some user-friendly Bibles, cards that say "Jesus loves porn stars" (it's true, you know), and—this is key—our belief that the God in us is greater than the sin that surrounds us.

That's the question we always get: "How do you guys do it?" We're able to go to our gutter because we aren't scared of it. Too many Christians get scared of the world, but when you look at Jesus and the things He did, the way He brought light into darkness, you can plainly see that we have nothing to be scared of. I go to a trade show, and all I see are a bunch of miserable, unhappy people. People looking to fill their lives with this crap that's leaving them empty. I'm happily married. I don't want what they have; they want what I have.

So for now, that's my gutter, redefined. I'm called to go into the pornography gutter and bring the light of Christ with me. What's your gutter? What's your version of the porn show gutter? Where in the real world are you called to take Christ's light? Is it your workplace? Your school? Your home?

You can't be afraid of the world, and you can't be afraid of the reaction from the Church. Mike and I and the rest of the XXXchurch team haven't abandoned our faith in the least bit, but we have angered many people in the Church just by going into such an extreme gutter. More of them are on board with our mission now, but you wouldn't believe the flack we caught when we first started.

Hear this—we saw so much resistance, we began to question our calling. We wondered if we were making the right decision, and for just a moment, we lived in that shaky place where we weren't sure we'd heard God for real. Perhaps you've been there? While resistance made us question our calling, we didn't forfeit it. We had to make some bold choices and take some bold steps, but we did it because we wanted to remain true to God's calling on our lives and true to the gutter we needed to step into. It was intimidating and exhilarating at the same time. But that's sometimes the way it goes when you follow God.

# 03
# HANGING OUT IN THE GUTTER

## CHAPTER THREE

We started XXXchurch at a porn show, but we had no idea that we would attract attention from other gutters. Early in our development, we heard from a guy named Bill Day, a documentary filmmaker who wanted to follow us around for a bit and see what he got on film. Eager to spend some time in other gutters, and somewhat flattered at his request, we said, "What the heck," and agreed, figuring Bill would be around us for a week or so, maybe a month at most. We had no idea what we were in for.

Two and a half years later, Bill finished a feature documentary on the ministry of XXXchurch.com. What began as a lark turned into a two-and-a-half-year odyssey. The big story here isn't about us; it's about Bill. Bill is a gutter resident, a non-Christian, and a really great guy. I have to admit; having him around pointing a camera at us was great motivation for us to stay on our toes.

During that time, Bill was an inspiration to us. We had an awesome time just hanging out in the gutter with this guy, never preaching or beating him over the head with some sermon, but instead just living our faith in front of him. He saw that we were humans who have flaws and who make mistakes, but who still have a deep, abiding faith in Christ, and that faith drives us in everything we do.

Look, I'd like to say our ministry intrigued Bill, but that wouldn't be true—he started out making a movie about porn. But the more time he spent with us, the less the film became about porn and the more it became about our faith. (The film, called *Missionary Positions*, is scheduled to be released in 2005. Check *www.missionarypositions.tv* for more info.) Bill wanted Mike and I to essentially narrate the whole movie, so toward the end of the project, he spent a lot of time with us one on one, going over different voice-overs and lines for the narration.

I remember one night when we just kept shooting and shooting and shooting. It was getting late, but Bill assured me we were almost done. Then in the midst of my tiredness, he said, "Talk about what drives you and why you keep pressing on in this ministry, despite all the hard times you've faced."

He pointed the camera at me, and the first thing that popped into my head was Matthew 17:20, where Jesus said, "If you have faith as small as a mustard seed, you can say to this mountain, 'Move from here to there' and it will move. Nothing will be impossible for you."

"Cut." Bill put the camera down, smiled, and said it was great. Incredible. PERFECT. And I remember so clearly the gutter-bred line he said next: "S---, where did you get that from? That's really from the Bible?"

The camera was off; nobody was watching, no permanent record of what happened next. Bill and I began to talk about faith that can move mountains, and Bill began to understand just a little bit more about the God I serve and what that God is capable of doing.

I saw the movie at a special screening in Hollywood last week, and that scene is still in there. But here's the kicker—that Bible passage isn't just in the movie; I believe it plays a big part in the development of this film. That little scene captures more of our faith than Bill ever set out to capture in the first place. More important than whether my "perfect" quotation scene is in the movie or not—that verse has stuck with Bill and caused more searching and questioning about this God I serve.

I love Jesus' last recorded words here on earth. In Mark 16:15, just four verses before He ascending in heaven, Jesus tells the disciples to "go into all the world and preach the good news to all creation." Growing up in the Christian ghetto, I heard these words so many times that they lost their meaning. I heard it analyzed this way by this speaker and that way by that speaker. I discussed it in small groups and was lectured on it in big groups. And I forgot something really simple in the midst of it all.

When Jesus said, "Go," what He meant was, "Go."

It's perfectly plain—as a Christian, I'm supposed to go into the world. Not just the Church, not just the Christian ghetto—the *world*. To the gutters and alleys and seedy places or, sometimes, to jail.

The Apostle Paul was familiar with that—jail. He wrote Ephesians while in a prison cell, and he said something very revealing about himself and God in Ephesians 3:7-8:

> This is my life work: helping people understand and respond to
> this Message. It came as a sheer gift to me, a real surprise, God
> handling all the details. When it came to presenting the Message
> to people who had no background in God's way, I was the least

qualified of any of the available Christians. God saw to it that I was equipped, but you can be sure that it had nothing to do with my natural abilities. And so here I am, preaching and writing about things that are way over my head, the inexhaustible riches and generosity of Christ (MES).

Paul knew something many people in the Church don't know—God called him to do what he had to do, and then God gave him the ability to do it. That's just the way God works. He wouldn't call you to do something and then leave you high and dry when it came to actually doing it. He wants you to carry out His plan, not be frustrated.

The problem is that so many people, maybe even you, don't believe this. They just don't think it is actually possible to go into all the world and preach the good news. They think they don't have what it takes to go into the gutter, so they play it safe and stay in the Christian ghetto.

This may sound a bit crude, but bear with me. When a baby is born, one of the first things it does is have a bowel movement. The parents don't have to teach it how to go; the baby doesn't have to study it or think about it—it just goes. What is in that baby will eventually come out of that baby. The same applies to you. Not to be sacrilegious, but if you're a follower of Christ, the Spirit is in you and wants to help get God's gifts out of you and into the real world. God promised He'd give you the power. It won't always be easy out there, and you'll have your share of setbacks and frustrations (I know I have), but God will always be there with you, giving you the power to keep going.

You know what I hear all the time when I go to speak at churches or conferences? "I could never do what you're doing." You know what I say? Usually I say something like, "Well, I understand. This is what God has called me to do."

You know what I *want* to say? "Why not? Stop being so weak. God did not create you to be a scared, irrelevant Christian. Why can't you do this? What is holding you back if you know what God's Word says and you know what He's capable of doing? Whywhywhy?! Stop being afraid of the gutter and just go get in it." The world looks at the Church and sees a bunch of people too afraid to approach them.

If we'd approach the gutter—really approach it—we'd be surprised at what we'd find. Two years after we started XXXchurch, James DiGiorgio, a famous pornographer of fifteen years, sent me an email that contained a link to his popular weblog. I checked out the link and read this post:

> To some of you, this might sound like I've lost it, but I've decided to make an offer to the XXXchurch that they probably CAN refuse ... but who knows?

> Maybe you've heard of the XXXchurch? They're the people who produced and are airing anti-porn commercials. The "hook" (or theme) has to do with their message about porn stunting your growth.

> I'm not sure if porn actually stunts anyone's growth—actual, psychological, emotional, or spiritual—at least in terms of the viewing of porn stunting one's growth. I am quite sure, however, that producing porn stunts some of your s---, especially after producing it for a long time. I know it has stunted me—most assuredly psychologically. But I was probably stunted in more ways than I care to admit before I got into porn so what the f---. I'm also fairly sure there are porn fans out there who are obsessed with watching this stuff we make. And getting obsessed about anything usually has stunting consequences, in one way or another. But that's their problem, not mine.

Anyway, I went to XXXchurch.com and checked out what these particular anti-porn Christians had to say. And while I can't say I'm ready to see the light, I'll admit these people don't come off as whacko zealots. And they seem to have a sense of humor and a penchant for the offbeat (as indicated by their kung fu Jesus T-shirt).

So here's the deal: I'm an equal opportunity kind of guy. I so firmly believe in the 1st Amendment that I'll support these XXXChurch guys with as much ardor as I support what we do here in the jizz biz regardless of the fact that these XXXChurch guys would rather see me and all of us in the adult world go belly up.

So in the non-spiritual spirit of getting the word out ... make that getting their word out (whether I agree with it or not), I'd like to volunteer my time and resources to helping the XXXChurch make their next anti-porn commercial.

That's right, I'm willing to shoot and edit their next thirty-second spot for free. I'll supply the cameras, lights, sound equipment, and crew at no cost to them. I'll shoot and direct and perform the editing for absolutely no charge.

Call me crazy. Call me a turncoat. Call me whatever the f--- you want. I don't really give a s---. I got my own reasons for making this offer and frankly, my reasons are no one's business but my own. So now I'm going to write an email to these guys and make my offer to them. I'll let you know what they say.

In case you're wondering if you read that correctly, let me reiterate. James DiGiorgio, a veteran pornographer, volunteered his time, resources, and energy to make a thirty-second commercial for us.

Of course, we took him up on it.

His friends and coworkers call him Jimmy D., and he's fairly prolific, from a pornography standpoint. He's directed more than a hundred porn films, so we figured he must know his way around a camera. Besides, he presented us with the perfect opportunity to showcase Jesus' love in the gutter.

After that first porn show, we got tons of press. We could have taken that notoriety and split, patting ourselves on the back for our successful trip into the gutter. But we didn't. We kept going back, and we met Jimmy D. at one of those subsequent porn shows. His booth was across the way from ours, so we got to spend some time with him, and he got to see that we were for real.

Jimmy D. sent us that email, fully expecting us to laugh it off and say, "No thanks." He'd encountered Christians before and knew the drill. He definitely wasn't thinking that we'd jump at the chance to utilize his services; maybe he wound up getting more than he'd bargained for. In his email to us, he even said, "I understand if you do not want to work with me and take me up on this offer."

Our relationship with Jimmy D. was so important to us that we stayed in his personal gutter. We first met at that porn show; the second time we met to talk about our commercial, we offered to come to his studio—to his turf—to talk about it. Soon we found ourselves in the middle of Jimmy D.'s gutter, sizing up his studio and deciding what our commercial should be about.

We filmed the commercial, a puppet-based spot aimed somewhat at children, but more toward hip-thinking adults, and during that time we struck up a great relationship with him. Suddenly the world started watching us. The story of two pastors forming a working relationship with a known pornographer made national news. We intended on taking the light of Christ into Jimmy D.'s darkness, and wound up taking it to the whole world in the process. Before we knew it, our "Pete the Porno Puppet" commercial was being aired on televisions—via news programs—all over the country.

Our story was told by: CNN, FOX, ABC News, *The Daily Show*, *Newsweek, People, GQ, USA Today*, and *The Los Angeles Times*.

And more than one hundred news agencies around the world. In the end, more than 100 million people heard our story and saw part of the commercial. Why? A ton of TV spots are produced every week, but one made headlines. There was just something about the idea of two pastors working with a veteran pornographer that news producers couldn't pass up. The *L.A. Times* story said it best in its simple title: "Unlikely Bedfellows."

People were wondering, "What are two pastors doing with a porn director?" They thought our alliance went against everything we stood for, but they thought wrong. In actuality, working with Jimmy D. is the perfect example of *everything* we stand for. Frankly, all the hoopla about our relationship is a sad commentary on the Church's performance when it comes to getting in the gutter. This type of thing is exactly what Christians *should* be doing, but the only reason we made so much news is because most Christians aren't doing it.

Ironically, despite the overwhelming interest from the mainstream media, hardly anyone in the Christian media covered this story. We were good enough for CNN, but not TBN. (Granted, we did get a mention on *The 700 Club*, but it was after a battle with them, and it aired on Pat Robertson's day off, since he didn't approve of our ministry methods.) So why didn't we get a ton of buzz in the Christian world? I think it's because many of the people in the Christian media are scared. They think we went too far. That we're becoming "of the world," so to speak.

Probably because this commercial was the most high-profile thing we'd ever done, it easily became the most controversial thing we'd ever done. We lost support and started getting barrels of hate mail. Honestly, I don't understand why the Church at large would react this way. Jimmy D. is searching. Like everyone else in the gutter, he's there because he's lost, and whether he knows it or not, he's searching for something and someone to help get him out of the gutter. I believe as Christians we have to be willing to climb down in there and associate with gutter residents—we have to get a little dirty in order to help the Jimmy D.s of the world out.

Don't get me wrong, here. I don't want Jimmy D.'s life. I love my life and my relationship with Christ. But I don't think my faith is meant only for me—it's something I'm supposed to share with and show to the rest of the world, including veteran pornography producers like James DiGiorgio, or unsaved guys like Bill Day—who see what I have and realize how integral it is to my life.

I've talked a lot about Jimmy D., but so far I haven't really shown you the world as he sees it. Here's an excerpt from one of his website entries where he talks about his "to-do" list for the next day. See if you can relate to any of this.

> HERE'S JIMMY'S LIST: whatever day you're reading it:
> 1. Wake up.
> 2. Wake up again after falling back asleep right after the first time I woke up.
> 3. Take a piss.
> 4. Stumble down the stairs to the kitchen and make coffee.
> 5. Wake up again after falling back asleep in a chair waiting for the coffee to brew.

6. Check out whatever bulls--- is on the web while sipping my cup-o-Joe.
7. Wake up again after falling back asleep.
8. Take a dump.
9. Take a shower.
10. F--- around on the web some more while my hair dries.
11. Wake up again after falling back asleep waiting for my hair to dry.
12. Get dressed.
13. Drive to the Valley to deliver this CD of images I forgot to burn on the last set I was on.
14. Shoot a scene.
15. Go to a couple of different banks to see if a couple of different checks I've been carrying around are finally good.
16. Stop at the Goodwill and see if there's any more junk I want to buy to further clutter my living environment.
17. Stop at the grocery store and pick something up to eat when I get home.
18. Arrive home, eat whatever I picked up, head to my room and my computer and my stereo and my DVD player and my TV and play everything simultaneously while I surf the net.
19. Get stoned.
20. Maybe write some lame s--- for this site.
21. Climb into bed and fall back asleep while trying to remember what I have "To Do" the next day.

Man! What an exciting life, huh?

See, Jimmy D. is a normal, lost guy trying to make it through the day, just like everyone else in the gutter. Just like many Christians. Change his career and he could be a sibling, relative, parent, co-worker—anyone. Ultimately, he's just another guy in the gutter, looking for something to add a little meaning to his life, wasting his talents in the world instead of using them for God.

We had a premiere for *Missionary Positions* not too long ago, and just after the movie started, in walked Jimmy D. But not Jimmy D., the porn producer. This was Jimmy D., the father and grandfather. He escorted his twenty-one-year-old daughter while holding his one-month-old grandson. There's a part of the movie that features Jimmy D. on the set, and it is by far the most shocking and revolting part of the movie. It's just Jimmy doing his job, but it's pretty upsetting to see him at work.

So most of the people probably got a notion of what Jimmy D. was like based on that footage in the movie. But when the film was over and the lights came up, people got to see Jimmy D. for who he really is. Just a normal guy with a child and a grandchild. People began to see him as God sees him. He isn't a porn producer—he's a lost child of God. This is how we need to see people in the gutter.

I mentioned earlier that we appeared on *The 700 Club*, and it actually turned out to be a really interesting piece. When they asked if they could do a story on us, I told them I would only do it if they let me bring my new friend Jimmy D. with me. They agreed, and so did Jimmy D., who has a great sense of humor. (Funny thing—when we met him and worked with him, he had long hair; he showed up to tape this interview for *The 700 Club* with a brand new short haircut. He said he did it for his mom; I think he did it for Pat Robertson.)

You can watch the piece on our website (*www.xxxchurch.com/patrol/commercial.asp*), and Jimmy D. has some interesting things to say in it. His first impression of us: "Oh, I get it. You guys are like Jesus walking among the lepers." He even admits that he thinks we're "great guys and fun to hang out with."

The reporter, Paul Strand, asked Jimmy D. if we were "getting through to him." In his typical fashion, Jimmy D. took the no-nonsense approach. "I'm sure you and your viewers would love to have me say, 'Yes,' but unfortunately, 'No.' I feel the faith that they have, I can sense that ... it's a real thing, it's almost a tangible thing."

Really, that's all Mike and I can ask for. After hanging out at the studio, shooting the commercial, and doing multiple days of press interviews, Jimmy D. has seen our faith and knows it is what drives us. I believe he saw it when he first met us, and that's one of the reasons he emailed us in the first place.

Can I be honest? One of the things that really bugs me about that report is the way they cap off the Jimmy D. story. I'm thankful for the exposure and all, but they cut right from Jimmy D. saying he isn't a "convert" to a mention of our website. You know what the reporter says there? "The website has been much more successful, some 30 million hits so far."

Did you see that? The implication is that our work with Jimmy D. isn't successful because he hasn't come to the Lord yet. What is wrong with this picture? If you go to the gutter, you have to be willing to stay in the gutter. Our Christian mentality is to visit the gutter over spring break or during a summer missions trip. But to live there and hang out there, to hang around people who live in the gutter ... YES, YES, YES.

Jimmy D. said, "I have seen their faith, I know that drives them, but I am not a believer," so in the eyes of *The 700 Club*, that's failure. NO, NO, NO. If you decide to venture into the gutter, know what you are getting into. Know that this isn't just a quick trip. It isn't just a chance to take a peep around, throw out some Gospel tracts, and then head home. If that's your mindset, then please don't even go at all.

If we got some people saved at the porn shows we attend, we'd have more fans. If Jimmy D. became a Christian, more people would like us. But I look at the gutter differently. Gutter residents aren't notches on a Bible or marks on a Christian scorecard—they are real, hurting people, people who are so lost they'll break your heart. Most of the time it takes more than a Gospel browbeating to help them realize their plight.

A friend of mine, Jeff, once summed it up perfectly for me: "Don't blame the dark for being dark. Blame the light for not shining on the dark."

Think about some potential gutters you can reach, some dark places where your light can shine. If you really think about it, think about your skills, your life experience, and your calling, then you'll be able to identify what your gutter is and where you need to be reaching. You don't need me to point you in one specific direction—you know where your gutter is. The bigger question is: Are you looking for it?

# 04
# THE GUTTER
# GETS DIRTY
## CHAPTER FOUR

Can I tell you a secret? Maybe I'll just ask you a question. Now, I've hinted at this already, so if you get this right, consider yourself a good detective: Where do you think Mike and I have received the strongest opposition to our ministry? Was it from the Church or from the gutter?

Of course, you know the answer. We get so much flak from so many Pharisaical Christians for what we do, but to that, I say this: Yes, the gutter is dirty and messy and full of the unknown, but then again, so is life. Anyone who tells you any different is selling something.

Nine months after we started XXXchurch, we put up a billboard on one of the local highways, but the complaints of the religious forced us to take it down after just one month. Since we'd blown $4,000 on just that one billboard, we decided to advertise a different way—with something no one could take down. We got a car. Not just a car, but the hip, new Toyota Scion XB. Then we wrapped it up in some rad XXXchurch.com graphics and voilà—our very own driving billboard. We call it the "Porn Mobile."

Shortly after the Porn Mobile came into being, my wife Jeanette and I, along with our then-nine-month-old son Nolan, drove it to one of the most progressive churches in California. I have some friends who attend regularly, and we thought now would be a good time to check out the service and bring along the Porn Mobile for its maiden voyage. We parked without incident, attended the service, and prepared to head home. My wife went to the nursery to pick up Nolan and then headed to the car to feed him while I stayed behind to talk to one of the church's men's group leaders.

She took off for the Porn Mobile, but when she got there, she found it surrounded by three people, a note on the windshield. She snatched the note up and read it: "You are more than welcome to come back to this church, but please do not park the car here or bring the car at all." Nice welcome.

At this point, my wife decided to carry out her mission of feeding Nolan, but as she tried to get into the car, one of the three people surrounding it began harassing her. He kept telling her that "XXX" is a dirty word and therefore should be taken out of the slogan, while she kept telling him that it was a good thing, trying to explain our mission. Aware that the whole encounter was going downhill fast, my wife finally just got in the car and started with the feeding.

A different man came over to talk with the guy who'd originally started hassling Jeanette. After hearing she was in the car, he started harassing her by pounding on the window. Well, by this point Jeanette was pretty upset and tried to call my cell phone so I could come rescue her.

Unfortunately I'd turned it off during the service (note to the PowerPoint announcement people: Those reminders to turn off your cell phone really do work) and hadn't turned it back on. She was officially stuck.

Things settled down, and the people finally went away. After she was done feeding and Nolan had a full tummy, Jeanette got out of the car to come find me. As she walked through the parking lot, one of the attendants tracked her down and told her the police were on their way. Someone had called them and complained about the Porn Mobile, and now the long arm of the law was getting involved.

It was getting surreal. What happened next interested me the most. The window-pounding guy saw my wife talking to the parking lot attendant (who was relieved to hear what we were about). He interrupted them to start an argument. My wife tried to brush the window pounding guy off, but he was persistent in his attack. And you know what he kept saying to her? "I don't want to discourage you from coming back to our church, BUT ..." I can't think of a *less* loving thing to say to a person.

All this over a stupid car.

In a *church* parking lot.

So, while all this was going down, I was having a lovely chat. I'd even mentioned the Porn Mobile to the guy I was talking to, and he wanted to come see it. He had other business to attend to first, so I told him where we parked and then headed out the door to meet up with Jeanette. When I got there, I found out all that had gone on and started laughing at the absurdity of it all (though I felt bad that this had happened to my wife). Of course, Jeanette didn't find it funny.

The parking lot attendant informed me of the police involvement and suggested we just hop in the ol' Porn Mobile and hightail it out of there.

Call it pride, call it righteous indignation, call it just plain stubbornness, but I wasn't having any of that. We stood our ground and stuck around to see what would happen. Sure enough, the police came. Secretly, I was hoping they'd try to handcuff the Porn Mobile—it would've made a great page on our website.

Finally, salvation—the men's leader I'd been talking to earlier came out from the church. He saw all that was going on, shook his head in disgust, ripped up the note, and apologized to us profusely. The parking lot circus disbanded, and we all went our separate ways.

Crazy, but true. And although it seemed lighthearted at the time, the experience began to sink in as we piloted the Porn Mobile home. What if I were a porn producer, involved in this filthy XXX industry? What if I were searching for God and had driven my company's vehicle to church as I sought Him? Shouldn't the church embrace and welcome me no matter what I do, what I look like, or what kind of car I drive? Shouldn't they be thrilled that a true seeker was paying a visit? What if I'd let my friend Jimmy D. drive the car to church that day?

In Luke 5:31-32, Jesus said (I'm paraphrasing here), "Healthy people don't need a doctor—sick people do. I have come to call sinners, not those who think they are already good enough."

Have we become too healthy in our churches? The Porn Mobile incident didn't happen at what most people would consider a "legalistic" church, which makes me wonder if something like that could happen at almost any church.

A funny thing about these types of Christians is that they're equal-opportunity offenders. They're just as comfortable offending people *off* church property as they are *on*. One of the strangest opponents we've ever met is a guy we've dubbed "Pastor Bible." I already talked about how we go to pornography trade shows as part of our ministry, and we're getting pretty good at it. After our first show in Las Vegas, we started getting invitations to come to other shows, and we got invited to Erotica L.A., so we went. By our fourth porn show in two years, we felt like we were making some progress and giving some of the people there a new understanding of what the Gospel looks like.

Then people started saying to us, "Oh, you're just like the guys standing outside." Well, of course, we had no idea what they were talking about, so we headed outside to have a look.

Outside, we found a couple of guys with big signs that had slogans like, "The Unbelieving, Abominable, Murderers, Whoremongers, Sorcerers, Idolaters, and All Liars will burn in HELL (Rev. 21:5)," "Read the BIBLE while you're able (Matt. 4:4)," and my personal favorite, toted by Pastor Bible himself, which said "REPENT OR PERISH" on one side and "JESUS SAVES FROM HELL" on the other side, both signs complete with artistically drawn fire at the bottom.

But while the other gentlemen held only signs, Pastor Bible was equipped with a bullhorn, and he was using it to berate everyone who walked into the show. (It was really quite a sight, and you can see a clip of it on our website at *xxx.church.com/involved/video_audio.asp*—just scroll down and watch the video labeled "Amazing Grace: Erotica LA 2003.") I couldn't believe the things that were coming out of this man's mouth. He had complete disdain for everyone walking into that building, calling everyone "stupid" and "slow-minded" and preaching his message of fear. He said, "The Bible talks about loving God, but you know what it talks about more? Fear. Fear ... You need to be terrified of the God of the Bible, for what He's going to do to you for what your actions are—Hey, get your hands off that, pig!"

He objected to my attempt to plug his bullhorn with my hand.

I'm sure Pastor Bible had good intentions (at least, I *hope* he did), but he was going about *his* mission all wrong. He was trying to reach the gutter on his terms, terms that included the fear of God and hard-core repentance. But Jesus was a genuine lover of people, and everyone flocked to Him because He met needs, not because He preached about the kingdom of heaven. He met needs first as a practical way of showing that He loved the people, *then* got into the meatier theological issues. Pastor Bible would have it the other way around.

Ironically, one of the porn actresses walking into Erotica L.A. had a clearer picture of Christ than our sign-toting friends. Walking past our cameras as we filmed Pastor Bible, she looked over her bikini-top-clad shoulder and said, "I believe Jesus loves everyone."

So many Christians use misguided attempts like these to steer the lost out of the gutter, but they so often fail. It's just human nature to want to do the exact opposite of what you're told to do, especially if you're being told to do it by someone with a bullhorn. Even Adam, given a direct order by God, ate the *one piece of fruit* he was told not to eat. Since we have a sin nature, a fleshly desire, we tend to want to do what is wrong and head into our various gutters, no matter what they might be.

While the Church at large is great at telling people to avoid their gutters, I've found that this approach just doesn't work anymore. Actions used to be generational—kids would do exactly what their parents did because that's just the way things were; family businesses were passed down from generation to generation to generation. Things have changed, and people don't do things just because they're told to do them or because those things are expected of them.

So we as a Church have to change our approach and get dirty. Modern Christians must take risks and get out of their comfortable pews and classrooms and do something for God. If we don't, who will? Pastor Bible? I pray not.

I hate to break this news to the Pastor Bibles of the world, but a lot of people just aren't interested in church anymore! At least not in the traditional pews-and-hymns sense. So it's up to us to take the church to them, and that's why Mike and I were at the porn show. That's why we do everything we do.

As long as I'm breaking bad news, here are some statistics you probably don't want to hear: Of Americans in their mid-twenties to early-thirties, only 28 percent regularly attend church, and that number dwindles when you look at people between eighteen and twenty-four, with only 8 percent regularly attending. Eight percent! A generation ago, half our parents and grandparents were dutiful churchgoers, but now young, single, and well-educated adults are the *least* likely group of people in the United States to attend church. By the year 2010, 100 million people who went to church this Sunday will no longer be going.

We must do something, or the Church will not be able to continue thriving like it has in the past. What can we do? If you've read any part of this book already, you'll know the answer is obvious to me—we must get in the gutter. Think about it. Where do lost people—the people we need to reach in order to grow our congregations—spend most of their time hanging out? Is it in the Church? Of course not! But instead of going to them, most churches meet and meet and meet some more; pray with Christians, sing with Christians, live with Christians, and eat with Christians.

What is it about the gutter that makes us so afraid?

The world as we know it is a dark place, and Jesus told us to take His light into this dark place. While the mission couldn't be simpler, I've noticed that many of us in the Church would rather sit back and criticize what others do instead of actually doing something ourselves. But this wasn't the way Jesus worked, and it shouldn't be the way the Church works either.

## CHAPTER FOUR

Not too long ago I was a guest on a nationwide Christian radio talk show, and the host had a problem with XXXchurch, saying our intentions might be good, but if we got too close to the fire we would eventually get burned. I was outraged. Instead of talking about our ministry and how much success we've had in the gutter, I had to spend the whole hour defending my beliefs and the things we've done. The host wasn't interested in the success of XXXchurch; he had his own agenda and opinion on what Christians should or should not do to reach out to people, and he strongly believed what we were doing was not the right way.

This type of behavior is symptomatic of a larger disease in the Church. Shortly after my radio appearance, we received an email from a guy named Charles Smith, who was a youth ministry volunteer and a huge supporter of our ministry. He told us his story and how he had just recently been let go from his position for passing out information about XXXchurch. His email closed with this:

> I wanted you guys to know that I think what you guys are doing is the greatest, most forthright effort I have seen to date. I believe what you are doing is the most needed ministry in the world today. Sexual immorality is the biggest, most dangerous, most deceptive struggle confronting society to date. I let my church know in no uncertain terms that the bold effort of our senior staff to censor me is a complete failure. I told him the only way they could stop me would be to excommunicate me. I love you guys, and my prayers are with you. Never stop fighting the good fight, whatever the cost.

Here's the question: Whom is Charles fighting? Whom are we fighting? Are we fighting to win the world for Christ? Or are we just fighting among ourselves in the church? Are we too much about getting fed and too little about exercising our faith? Yes, we keep fighting the good fight, but must we fight our brothers and sisters in Christ? No one wins that way. Why can't we all put our focus on the lost, those living in the dark places, the "whosoevers" who are so close to Christ's heart?

The day after we got that email from Charles, Mike and I received a phone call from cable channel TechTV wanting us to be guests on a show called *Unscrewed*. Now when we talk about getting in the gutter, *Unscrewed* is in the gutter. Hosted by a lovable goofball named Martin Sargent, it's a late-night talk show that's sort of a tech version of *The Tonight Show*, complete with skits, guests, and other funny bits related to things found online—including a "free porn tip of the day."

We flew into San Francisco to tape the show and had a blast on the air. We got a chance to talk about some of the different ministries we have on our site, and they showed one of our television commercials in its entirety. The studio audience was lively and intrigued, and the co-host, Laura, even took our "NoHo Pledge" (a solemn promise for women to dress a little more modestly and to stop looking like, well, hos) right there on TV. So all in all, we had a fun time.

No big deal, right? Just a standard television appearance—until you compare it to my interview on the Christian radio show. There, all I got to do was defend my beliefs to Christians—for a whole hour. Our segment on *Unscrewed* ran just about seven minutes. Guess which appearance sent more people to our website and therefore to our ministry. If you head to the gutter and are honest and real about who you are and why you're there, people will respond.

And then there was the Church rearing its ugly head again and telling us we shouldn't be involved in that type of television. We really took some shots when we showed up on *The Daily Show* and in the pages of *GQ* magazine. And I'm not saying this as some sort of "Check me out, look how cool and famous I am" type of nonsense. I mean: I'm the last guy I would ever expect to be in *GQ* (well, second-to-last guy, next to Mike). I'm just making the point that if you go to the gutter and are willing to risk getting dirty, you can sometimes wind up making a bigger impact on a larger stage.

So, the choice is yours. Do you really want to get dirty and get in the gutter, or do you want to play it safe and keep clean? Here's an email we received the day after our appearance on *Unscrewed*. Let it be an encouragement to you.

> OK, now that I have my breath back. What an incredible site and movement you have going. Bold. Outrageous. Shocking. Eye-opening. I'm still a little shaken. I found your site from TechTV and I'm glad I did. We need this. All of us who have struggled along the way and have tried and failed to bring the issue of porn to the forefront in the church need your kind boldness and courage to get back into the fray. Thanks. I have already emailed the site's address to a close friend of mine who also happens to be a youth pastor to get his read on it. I'm sure he will appreciate it as much as I have. The few shaky moments I spent looking through xxxchurch.com have reminded me of the love and passion I once had for Christ, and as I type this, admit I have lost in the past year. I truly believe that He led me to your work for a reason. I'll be in touch. Thanks for listening (to Him and me).

It's a dirty place, the gutter. But it's worth it.

# HIS GUTTER

## SECTION TWO

# 05

## THE GOD FROM THE GUTTER

### CHAPTER FIVE

The local church today must rediscover its primary purpose, and to do that, we must take a detailed look at the past, into the gene pool that produced Jesus. It's a colorful past filled with mistakes; David, for example, was a man who sinned several times over. And yet, despite his failures, he was still known as a man after God's own heart.

We find an interesting twist to the genealogy of Jesus further back in history with the mention of Rahab. This lonely woman was made great through one single action. A short story in the second chapter of Joshua describes how this street worker and gutter-dweller helped some men of Israel escape sure death.

On their way to the Promised Land, the Israelites had to conquer Jericho, a city of tremendous power and prestige, like an ancient Washington, D.C. Joshua, the commander of the Israelites, needed to know the lay of the land to assure a clear and clean victory, so he sent in some spies. Things went awry, and the local government detected the infiltrating Israelites, who tried to escape the city through the seedy part of town.

Burrowing through the Red Light District, they encountered Rahab, who decided to help them out and hide them on the roof of her house. The spies' pursuers showed up at her door, courtesy of the king of Jericho, but she cleverly led them astray and away from the Israelites. Once the pursuers left, she told the men how they could escape, and they got away safely.

Was she doing it for herself? No. She asked the men to show kindness to her family since she showed kindness to them, and because of her bold decision to do the right thing in that defining moment, her entire family—mother and father, brothers and sisters—were spared when Jericho fell (Josh. 6:22-23).

All in all, a nice story, something Hollywood producers would call a hooker-with-a-heart-of-gold tale. Except the story doesn't end there— this story produces truth from the gutter. This streetwalker's seed was a Savior; Jesus' ancestors were rooted in the gutter.

After Jericho was conquered, Rahab lived among the Israelites, traveling on to the Promised Land with them. She eventually married a guy named Salmon and had a child called Boaz, who we read about in the book of Ruth. Ruth and Boaz had a child named Obed, Obed and his wife had Jesse, and from Jesse came King David, the oft-sinning man after God's own heart. Leaping through some generations, we find that David was the great-great-great-great ... (twenty-four "greats" in all) grandfather of Joseph. Yes, the Joseph, as in Mary and Joseph.

Consider the implication here. Jesus, the savior of all mankind and the only sinless person ever to walk the face of this earth, has a prostitute in His family tree. Without Rahab, we'd never have had Jesus. Why would God use such a scenario to deliver His people? Why would He put the gutter squarely in the midst of the road to salvation? Simple. Because He knew all of us in need of deliverance would be just as messed up. There is no better way to communicate a compassionate love than to deliver the Savior through the gutter.

It could be any gutter. There is the gutter of substance abuse. The gutter of pain and bitterness. Or promiscuity. Or unforgiveness. God can and will use those who were abandoned to the gutter. The Bible speaks of this in 1 Corinthians 1:28, where the Apostle Paul writes, "He chose the lowly things of this world and the despised things—and the things that are not—to nullify the things that are." God will utilize the lives of the least of them. Despite a person's history, God always establishes a proactive plan of success. The only pre-qualification is a willing heart.

Who would've thought the Master's plan of a chosen Christ would come through the soiled Red Light District?

The irony of the situation is magnified by the inconsistent behavior of those He delivered: His Church. This is the very group that has been rightfully accused of largely abandoning those in the gutter.

Browsing through a college newspaper, I recently stumbled upon a brief article written by a student who had given up on the notion of a "loving" church, so much so that he titled his article, "Why Your Church Sucks." This frustrated and disillusioned person explained his perspective on how the Church is no longer relevant to hurting people. He believed authentic behavior had been lost because those in the Church had, in many cases, forgotten what it was like to be in the gutter, that their pasts, in their eyes, did not qualify for gutter status. Although I disagreed with his presentation, I agreed with his principle. Ultimately, his sorrow was rooted in the inconsistency embraced by many people in organized religion.

Maybe the typical church attenders aren't out of the Red Light District, the sex industry, a crack house, or a prison, but they are from the gutter. Maybe their gutter had a different circumstance and scenario. Maybe it was or is a deceitful business, a horrible marriage, an unavailable dad, or a sexually permissive wife ... we all have a gutter-filled past that we should not deny or forget. This is the very thing that defines our faith—that we no longer live in our gutters.

And it is the thing that should drive us back to the gutter. As Christlike people, unless we have gone to the gutter, we have not fully understood His purpose, nor fully embraced His plan for mankind. His plan is to make real love available to any and every person who would want it. When we understand Him, we will see what He sees.

This was made clearer to me recently when my friend Ramos told me a story. He and a team of gutter-goers were in San Francisco, assigned the task of mingling with the less fortunate in that area and sharing God's love with them. His team was handing out blankets that day, and had already finished up before the other teams arrived back at the ministry launch pad. Having some time to kill, Ramos decided to do some exploring. He crossed the street to try to grab a cup of coffee, and that's when he met Yo-Yo.

She was sitting next to the building asking for change, but the way she smiled captured his attention. Ramos asked her name and if she would like a cup of coffee. She gave the name, but politely declined the drink.

He went inside and ordered, but the irony of her name wouldn't leave him alone. Yo-Yo. A toy yanked up and down, drawn back and forth, then eventually discarded to the bottom of the toy chest. Yo-Yo was cold and alone. He returned to her on the corner and knelt down to strike up a conversation.

She told him she had been on the streets for more than two years, and when he asked her why, she paused before speaking the words that still ring in his ears. With a confused look but clear thought, she said, "Out here is better than at home."

My God! What must "home" have been like? To her, it was worse than the gutter.

Ramos invited her to join the concluding outreach only yards away and broke the entire set of street rules by giving her money so she could buy some food. Emotional, he staggered back to the ministry launch pad while she left to get something to eat. Although he had invited Yo-Yo back to the outreach, he did not expect her to show up, but twenty minutes after telling him the street was better than her home, she approached him as they packed their equipment.

They continued talking, and she told him that more than 90 percent of passers on the street ignore her existence. It occurred to Ramos that he had done the same. He had walked by "them," soothing his conscience with thoughts like, "If I give them money, they'll buy alcohol or cigarettes or ..."

The reality is that this time he could not ignore her and act as if she were not there. This was someone's daughter. God's daughter. Knowing she needed the practical warmth a blanket provides, he also realized she was in need of the kindled warmth that Christ provides. One should open the door for the other.

They searched through the remainders of their successful outreach and couldn't find a single blanket. Disappointment overwhelmed his new friend while the "daddy side" of his heart overwhelmed him. "What would I do to keep my own child warm if she were out on the street with me?" Ramos thought. He knew what he would do. If it were his daughter, he would shed his jacket without hesitation and see that her need was met. Even though Yo-Yo was not his daughter, she was his Father's daughter. She had tested positive as a legitimate, though rebellious, child of his King, his Dad.

Knowing that she was "family" moved Ramos to uncomfortable action in the gutter. He didn't take the time to justify or rationalize what he did, because he knew thinking would allow him time to reason away the most practical solution. Instead, he just took off his black jacket. Yo-Yo's eyes lit up. No tears, just an overwhelming smile expressing joy and warmth.

In that moment, he was warm.

Ramos introduced Yo-Yo to the local ministry team based in San Francisco. They talked and made arrangements for a continued friendship while he slipped away.

Later that night, he pulled into the driveway and felt the crisp air amplified. Ramos remembered this was the cold night temperature that blanketed Yo-Yo each night. But on this night, someone found a practical answer to a deep spiritual question. That answer is that we are called to love people, not judge people.

Does that sit okay with you? I know from experience that it's much easier to judge than to love. When we encounter the Yo-Yos of this world, we are faced with three questions to answer.

First, how do they impact us? Have we grown to be so desensitized that seeing a cold and hungry person no longer moves us? If we aren't challenged or moved when we come face to face with the gutter, then we are without compassion, which opens a bigger dilemma than the one opened by the gutter-dweller sitting in front of you. That dilemma: How can a Christlike person be unmoved by the pain of another? It is impossible to separate Christ and compassion; they are seamlessly braided together. They define each other. Christ is compassion, and compassion is Christ.

Secondly, if they impact us, what do we *think* we should do about it? I've found that usually people respond to situations like Yo-Yo's by finding a way to criticize the situation rather than deliver hope to it. Our minds have mastered this deceptive method, and it usually plays out like this: If I denounce this awkward situation as a social ill that is not my responsibility, then I can walk away with less guilt for not doing the right thing. Really. The more I bash the gutter, regardless of what that gutter looks like, the easier it is for me to ignore it. Conscience begins to negotiate us away from the problem. Phrases like "get a job" or "they'll spend it on drugs" flood our minds and silence the conviction of Christlike compassion. Compassion moves us toward the pain. We empathize. We embrace. We encourage. We equip. That's what Jesus did in the gutter, and we too must discover a way to provide a practical solution. To say "get a job" is to isolate the hurting person and make Christianity, and therefore Christ's claims, more unbelievable.

Jesus met physical needs before He asserted a spiritual answer, and if we are supposed to think and act like Christ, we will ask, "What is the best way for me to address the needs of this person God has allowed to cross my path?" If we stop to think about it, we will know how to help without dropping coins in a cup that we think will be used for drugs. We just have to use our minds.

First, how does it impact us? Second, what can we think of doing to assist? And the all-important third question: Will you act? It is one thing to be impacted and think of something to do; this third question is an entirely different question—a thing that takes guts to answer. Will you make a move to deliver someone from the gutter? The greatest propellant to get me to the gutter is my own memory and recollection. Making a proactive attempt to assist and love someone in the gutter is made easier when I remember that everyone, including myself, lived there once. Sure, I know, we were different. But regardless of what your gutter looked like, you too were once there, right along with me. But mercy came to us and evicted us from our past. Let Titus 3:1-8 be an encouragement to you.

> Remind the people to be subject to rulers and authorities, to be obedient, to be ready to do whatever is good, to slander no one, to be peaceable and considerate, and to show true humility toward all men. At one time we too were foolish, disobedient, deceived and enslaved by all kinds of passions and pleasures. We lived in malice and envy, being hated and hating one another. But when the kindness and love of God our Savior appeared, he saved us, not because of righteous things we had done, but *because of his mercy. He saved us* through the washing of rebirth and renewal by the Holy Spirit, whom he poured out on us generously through Jesus Christ our Savior, so that, having been justified by his grace, we might become heirs having the hope of eternal life. This is a trustworthy saying. And I want you to stress these things, so that those who have trusted in God may be careful to *devote themselves to doing what is good. These things are excellent and profitable for everyone.* (emphasis added)

Because of Jesus' mercy and His sacrifice on the cross, I have been rescued. We have all been saved, and now the rescued must become rescuer. There is no other option, especially when the Apostle Paul boldly tells us in this letter to Titus that we are to devote ourselves to what is good, because it is *excellent* and *profitable* for *everyone*. Jesus and His mission are all-inclusive.

No one who is aligned with Christ can find exclusion from this instruction. In fact, making a move to a person in the gutter is to make a move to the King of Creation. Remember, Jesus said that what we do to (what we consider) the least of our people, we "have done directly" to Him. To show them love is to show Him love; to isolate and ignore them is to isolate and ignore Him. It may be a paradox, but through this apparent contradiction comes the greatest clarity and spiritual freedom.

When we go to the gutter, we find the "whosoever" of John 3:16. When our eyes begin to see what God's eyes see, we are impacted. We think of a solution and make it happen more quickly. We go where He has already gone.

That which we do unto the least of them, we have really done unto Christ Himself. Here's the way I like to phrase it: If you haven't gone to the gutter, you haven't gone fully to Christ. After all, those in the gutter are the ones He called family, and the gutter is where He called home.

# 06
# THE GOD WHO LOVED THE GUTTER
## CHAPTER SIX

Nothing makes the Gospel of Jesus Christ more blessed or beautiful than His love for every sinner. Jesus said, "I came not to call the righteous, but sinners to repentance" (Luke 5:32). As He preached, the religious crowds were His worst enemies, but the sinners heard and embraced Him. He was (and is) the God who made a pitch for the impoverished people who are considered society's downtrodden. He negotiated for relationships with the least of us. He went to the gutter—and stayed there.

Like I've been saying—we have all experienced a gutter, and all our gutters look very different. A gutter to me may not be a gutter to you, but the bottom line is that we all are exposed to the gutters of life. A high-rise building full of corporate greed can be a gutter. It isn't just a poor man's venue; it isn't reserved for whores and pimps. The gutter is simply the place where disobedience comes to a dead end.

## CHAPTER SIX

The story of Zacchaeus in the first verses of Luke 19 is a perfect example of this aspect of the gutter, a New Testament story of restoration from the gutter of greed. The streets of Jericho (remember Jericho, home of Jesus' great-great-great-great-great (etc.) grandmother Rahab) bustled with business, and Zacchaeus the tax collector was in the middle of it all, skimming off the top and cheating the populace for ill-gotten gain. He lived in a relational gutter that flowed with social hatred. The residents of Jericho would see Zach coming and avoid him at all costs—they knew his intentions were always to extract money, so when Jesus and the multitude entered the city, Zacchaeus took notice.

Rumors of the recent miracles Jesus performed had spread like wildfire, so Zacchaeus had probably already heard that everywhere Jesus went, lives were changed. I'm guessing he thought Jesus would be good for a few bucks, being so popular and all. Lonely, socially isolated, and needing change but maybe not knowing it, Zacchaeus approached the crowd of people surrounding the Christ. Because of his short stature, Zacchaeus could not see past them. I assume he made an effort to see, craning his neck this way and that, hoping to get just a glimpse of this popular rabbi. But he couldn't see because of all the people following Jesus around.

Now, there has to be a reason this story is in the Bible. I'm sure Zacchaeus wasn't the first wee little man who climbed up in a sycamore tree to take a gander at the Messiah, so why did Luke feel the need to include him in this Gospel? I think a lot of it has to do with the multitude.

Think about it—here's a "lost person" trying to get a good angle on the Savior, but he can't get into a prime position because of all the people following Jesus, many of whom had probably already decided Jesus was the Messiah. But he is denied acceptance because of his reputation and because of his physical appearance. The same thing has happened over and over and over again on Sunday mornings in pews across our fruited plain. A lost person comes to church, only to be shunned, whether outright or implied, because of the way he looks or because of the emotional or spiritual baggage he carries.

I am guilty of this. I've seen it firsthand, and when I read Luke 19 with gutter-minded eyes, the realization of my previous actions painfully shoots through me. I asked myself the question of questions: Have my actions prevented a hurting person from getting a clear glimpse of Jesus?

I remember times I've clouded conversations with complex Christianese. I remember times when I've caused an unchurched person to shudder in disbelief at my hypocrisy. Or maybe my absence from the gutter has caused people to deny Christianity as a legitimate belief system. After all, Jesus made it clear that what we do to the least, we have done to Him. Using that literally in this story, Zacchaeus would be the least; he would've been Jesus. And he would've been boxed out.

Desperate and willing to forge his own destiny, the tax collector took off from the crowd. With sweat dripping from his face and his shortened legs sprinting ahead, Zacchaeus did the action that made him famous—he stopped and began to climb up into one of the trees that lined Jericho's streets. Inching out onto the limb, this prestigious tax collector must have looked undignified, but I doubt he really cared. He'd already admitted he *had* to see Jesus. As Jesus and the crowd approached, the masterpiece of gutter intervention was painted on the canvas of Zacchaeus' heart.

Jesus stopped. Without any apparent reason, Jesus looked up to the tax collector in the tree. I wonder what the crowd thought, or if they even noticed. Regardless, Jesus spoke out this "sinner's" name: "Zacchaeus, come down immediately. I must stay at your house today." You think Jesus had a little guidance from His Father on that one?

The Bible doesn't use the word "gasps" to note the reaction of the crowd, but you know they were heard. "What?!" "Did He just say that?!" "Doesn't

He know who that is?!" "He has gone to be the guest of a 'sinner'?!"

The religious wanted answers, but instead they got a lesson. Jesus had rolled up His sleeves and given the rest of humanity a lesson in Gutter 101. "Sinner," tax collector, churchgoer, pastor, pew-sitter, pimp, broken, abandoned ... Jesus made it very clear what His, and therefore our, mission is to be on earth. Our mission is to get in the gutter and provide Hope—even when that gutter is up on a tree branch over our heads.

And when Jesus turned toward the gutter, the gutter turned toward Him. It took all of two seconds for Zacchaeus to realize where his life had gone wrong. Instantaneously, he said, "Look, Lord! Here and now I give half of my possessions to the poor, and if I have cheated anybody out of anything, I will pay back four times the amount." Jesus reached into Zacchaeus' gutter, and Zacchaeus, in turn, reached out to Jesus.

Then Jesus spoke, and you can be sure the crowd was listening at this point: "Today salvation has come to this house ... for the Son of Man came to seek and to save what was lost."

That's love. When someone is willing to take a risk and love the unloved and unwanted—despite the assumptions and opinions of those around them—that's the love of Christ, plain and simple. It's the love we're supposed to show.

## LOVE IN THE GUTTER

The unconditional love of God is the only type of love that works in the gutter. It's a love that seeks to chase, find, and deliver those who are wandering. But there is a strange thing about the gutter. It makes me wonder: Why is something as pure as love the most profound thing in the lowest dwelling place? Where darkness abounds, love is brighter.

I once heard a story that painted a clear picture of this type of love to me. It's about a newlywed couple, and their lives are an incredible metaphor of God's love. Through their story comes a picture of true love for—and in—the gutter.

It's the story of a man of God, a God-chaser named José. José married his first love, and they soon had a child together. But as time passed, this newlywed wife became restless. The honeymoon was over; now their marriage had moved into more of a routine and was no longer blossoming with newness. The day-in/day-out sacrifice of mothering children was taking its toll, and her mind began to escape back to her past.

See, before she'd married José, she'd spent time in a sexual gutter. And now that gutter was looking pretty good. José knew about her past, but he loved her in spite of it, and he loved her still when she began to slip back into her old behavior. She began to seek fulfillment in the illicit and fleeting affection of an adulterous bed.

Soon she had another baby, and then another, neither of which were fathered by José. But the extra children didn't stop her—her wanderings in the night became more frequent. Each night after tucking her children into bed, she would slip out the back door and into the gutter, ready to sell herself to the highest bidder.

José was essentially alone, left to be a father to children that weren't biologically his, but he lovingly took up the task. In the mornings, he prepared them for the day, and many times as the boys finished breakfast, their mother would stumble through the door, exhausted from a night of hedonistic seduction. Soon, she quit coming home altogether.

As a husband, I can't imagine this. How could he allow her unfaithfulness to continue? How could he allow her to peruse the streets, a lustful lion seeking prey? If it'd been me, I would have put my foot down and taken control. Wouldn't you? Her prostitution and need for illicit gain only led her into slavery; she could not escape from the shackles of selfishness that kept her in the gutter. The chains of compromise gripped her so tightly she no longer considered the value of a husband and loving children.

She walked the streets each night to the marketplace to prostitute herself, to climb onto the auctioning block so men could bid for her affection. José sought God and saw her behavior as an invitation to the gutter, so, confused but obedient, José responded to God's call and made his way to the Red Light District. He didn't know what he was going to do there or what to expect, and when he finally arrived, what he saw crushed him. Imagine the pain and embarrassment he must have felt, seeing these men bid for his wife.

The man of God stood side by side with men of the world as they groped and placed bids for his beloved. And then he did a strange thing.

He placed a bid.

I know. It doesn't make sense. Why would he bid to purchase what already belonged to him—especially with the way she'd treated him and their children? To the gutter-blinded mind, it makes absolutely no sense, but from God's perspective, looking into the gutter, it's just what was called for.

As the men beside him sought a one-night stand, José sought his bride's faithful hand. "Ministry" in this environment would confuse the religious. This is not the type of outreach they teach in Bible college. But there were religious people there, people like Pastor Bible (remember him?). Folks from the local church, observing the drama unfolding, unaware of what was at stake. Hostile, yet hidden behind righteous indignations, the church people hurled condemning insults toward José.

Imagine the humiliation he endured as the religious scorned him for placing his bid. They thought it was a one-night stand, but they were wrong. It was gutter love.

That's what many religious people do. They stand on the sidelines, critical of situations that don't fit into their box of understanding. The Religious criticized everything Jesus did. Whether Jesus was on the road with Zacchaeus or in the temple with the Pharisees, they criticized and accused, seeking the worst. Instead, they found perfection. They couldn't believe a hay-filled manger in a smelly barn or a cruel timber on a garbage dump could produce a Messiah. They did not think these places could be the dwelling place of a Savior. The gutter simply did not fit into their box.

José stood nearly defeated and outbid. Wanting to finalize the transaction, he placed one last bid—all he had with him—fifteen dollars. The religious voices were dry from yelling. Raspy, ear-piercing, hate-filled voices filled the marketplace with judgment. The surrounding onlookers had to be shocked that a godly man was bidding on a whore. Of course, they didn't know it was his bride.

Prematurely aged by the gutter, the once-attractive young lady of earlier years had become worn and faded. But José wasn't bidding on her looks; he was bidding on her position. And he won. He bought his own wife at the auction of whores—for fifteen bucks. He sacrificed his pride and his money to bring her home—not as a slave, not as a prostitute, but as his wife, the lady of the house.

José's story can be repeated many times over. It applies to the Christian and the non-Christian, to the Jew and the Muslim ... to you and me. But while José's act was truly an example of the deepest kind of unconditional love, it was nothing new. God's always been involved with taking His love to the gutter, to the point of sending Jesus to the gutter of a garbage dump in order to create a bridge for mankind to get back to God.

Through Jesus on the cross, God bought back His most magnificent handiwork, an unfaithful creation that had sold out to the streets of selfishness. I am unfaithful. You are unfaithful. Every person that has ever breathed has been unfaithful. Each action I make contrary to God's plan for my life is an unfaithful act. Every time I go after money, power, my motive, my agenda, or self-fulfilling pleasures, *I am unfaithful to God*. Choosing to live in the gutter rather than to rescue people from the gutter makes me an unfaithful partner with God.

Each time I choose me, myself, and I—*my* agenda, *my* plan, *my* way—I throw myself into the arms and care of other gods, specifically, the god of self. The Bible refers often to this as "prostitution against God." (Check the Old Testament—God frequently uses prostitution or adultery as a metaphor for the children of Israel when they've turned away from Him.) Some think it's the worst sin in the Bible—worse than drugs, social injustice, homosexuality, or homicide. Of course, it isn't: no sin is worse than the next sin. Yet sin is sin, so there is no difference between the red-light dweller and penthouse-suite owner. There is no difference between the streetwalker and the religious person who condemns her. It's easily identifiable. I recognize it's the sin I commit the most and the sin I'm usually the last to confess.

The Bible insists again and again on the mercy of God. He is a God who is always waiting for me to recognize that I missed the mark. And when I make it right with Him by deciding to change and repent, He is ready to clean the slate, or, using José's story as an analogy, purchase me out of my unfaithfulness.

As much as the Bible has to say regarding the unfaithful, it also speaks of the severe punishments to the people of God who refuse to love the downtrodden. I see things like this in the Bible, and I ask myself the question over and over: How can I escape the gutter, only to be encouraged to go back with a desire to help the next person still dwelling there? These are the ones who have yet to turn from this unfaithful form of spiritual prostitution.

Sometimes our own unfaithfulness makes us unconcerned about those who live in society's gutter.

As José stood in the crowd watching other men battle for his wife, God must have revealed the reason he was there. No man in his right mind could have done what he did. If I were him, I probably would have argued with God. "What?! You want me to do what? This woman is in a covenant with me! Why should I buy back what already belongs to me?"

But José got it. "Lord, I see now. This is what you did for me. You loved me, even though I already belonged." To the church member, the choir member, the Sunday School teacher: We already belonged to Him. Yet because of our wanderings, because of our unfaithfulness, He had to buy us back. He brought redemption to us, and He paid for it Himself.

God bought us back. Not for a measly fifteen dollars, either, but with His own blood. He bought me off the bidding block and took me back into His home, not as a slave, but as a child of God, as one capable of receiving His inheritance! Now found innocent and faithful, you and I are brought into His presence as He prepares a feast for us. (Read the story of the Prodigal Son to get a great picture of how God the Father feels when His unfaithful kids come home: Luke 15:11-32.) How incredibly great is the love of God!

God is the God of José ... I mean Hosea. And it wasn't fifteen bucks; it was fifteen shekels and some barley. It wasn't last week or last year or last decade; it was nearly three thousand years ago, and it's right there in the Bible—Hosea 2:5 and 3:2. But regardless of the era, the plot remains the same: Unfaithful people who are desperate for the love a merciful, redeeming God will always find it. God is a God who loves the gutter, and He wants us to do the same.

The journey to the gutter pays great rewards in the form of transformed lives. We just have to get there.

# 07

# THE GOD WHO EMBRACED THE GUTTER

## CHAPTER SEVEN

Oh, man, do I get frustrated. Mention the word "Christian" to most people in our society, and chances are good you'll see them turn in disgust. Why does that frustrate me? Because *that's not how it's supposed to be.* After all, "Christian" is supposed to mean "little Christ," or more specifically, "Christ follower." So if Christians are really little Christs or followers of Him, why do so many unsaved people have such a bad taste in their mouths for the people of God? The unchurched and pre-Christian do not value the term "Christian."

But here's the ironic thing: In the days of the Bible, the ones who didn't like Jesus weren't the unchurched or irreligious ones. They were the religious. The Pharisees. The so-called church folks were the ones who despised Him. The Christians, though the disciples didn't call themselves that at the time, followed Him. The religious hated Him, and the unchurched hung out with Him whenever He was in town.

Three groups. Two sides. With Him or against Him.

The unchurched embraced Him then, but they don't now. So when did this spiritual reversal occur? When did the "lost" change their position? They didn't. We did. Christians did. Somewhere between the time Jesus ascended into heaven and now, we Christians, the walking billboards for Jesus' life-changing power, have done a lousy job of maintaining His momentum. Those who despise Him shifted too. The religious who once hated Him now advertise for Him. The lost who once hung out with Him now refuse to acknowledge Him. And it's all because Christians changed.

God didn't change. Jesus didn't change. His people did. At one point, the God who embraced the gutter was well represented. Jesus walked the streets and took an authentic love with Him—all the way to the gutter. Wherever He went, the unchurched responded while the religious scorned.

Fast forward two thousand years and now the reverse is true. Many Christians work endlessly to provide an authentic example of Christ's unfailing love. But often their message of Hope is corrupted from the outside by an overzealous Pastor Bible-type character who refuses to see people through love rather than law. When those who are "lost," or as I like to call them, "pre-Christians," see this judgmental display, they turn off their ears, and Christianity becomes unbelievable.

In the mid-'90s, dc Talk released its big hit record *Jesus Freak*, and while I in all my coolness have a difficult time admitting this, I kinda liked it. I especially liked the song "What If I Stumble," mainly because of the quote that precedes the actual song. The brief sound bite is a quote from author Brennan Manning, and he really just puts it all out there, painting a verbal picture of why a lost world finds little hope in Christians.

In case you've never heard the song or you don't remember and already sold this CD at your last garage sale, here's what he says: "The greatest single cause of atheism today is Christians, who acknowledge Jesus with their lips, then walk out the door and deny Him by their lifestyle. That's what an unbelieving world simply finds unbelievable."

Ouch. Hypocritical Christians have destructive effects—that hurts to hear. But while it's painful, in many cases, it's also true. Instead of loving and embracing those with a different spiritual opinion, we throw rocks at them to tear them down and elevate our position. Usually, the ones slammed with the rocks are the ones who need Jesus most.

I am reminded of a passage in the Bible where Jesus was faced with the same dilemma. It's found in John 8:1-11. Traveling with the disciples, Jesus made His way onto the sandy streets of the local marketplace. And then He saw her. In fact, there was no way He could have missed her, because she was headed toward Him, being dragged by the religious ones of the city. Most likely scantily clad and nearly nude, she was ceremoniously dumped at His feet, a woman who, according to John, had been caught in the very act of adultery.

The religious ones had apparently been out on Purity Patrol, and I guess their flesh-o-meter had gone berserk as they passed this woman's home. Did they peer in a window or just bust down the door? Who knows, but they caught the woman in the act and decided to use her sin as a way to trick Jesus and bring Him down. Being used—that's a lifestyle this woman probably found familiar.

(By the way, here's something I can't seem to shake: The Bible is clear that the woman's accusers had caught her in the act, which begs the question: Why were they watching? I realize this is purely speculation, but to me it sounds like the priests were partaking in some first-century porn, yet they still had the audacity to bring judgment on the one they'd been watching. They were guilty of the same act, but rather than admit it, they judged it.)

Imagine what must have been going on in her mind. Maybe that's a difficult request, but I'm not asking you to imagine yourself as a scantily clad adulterer. I'm asking that you think about being a person who has missed the mark, maybe for the hundredth time. Someone who has a perpetual problem with that thing that always trips them up. Not necessarily committing adultery or even having sex, but something else. Something like (this is where you fill in the blank with whatever secret sin you may or may not have, the one you never talk about. You know, *that* thing.)

Okay. So now you're thinking of that thorn in your side that you still engage in from time to time, even though you know it's wrong. And you're right in the middle of engaging in it when someone from the local church, maybe a deacon or an elder or the pastor's wife, drops in on you *in the very act* and takes it upon himself to drag you in for confrontation. Right then and there, without a chance to clean up or anything, you're dragged in front of your church on Sunday morning and an explanation is demanded of you.

Can you start to identify with this woman now? That's what she was dealing with, that's what she was feeling. Much worse than her skin, her sin had been exposed for all to see, and she was there, all alone, with no one to help her out. Not even the guy she'd just been sleeping with. Totally alone. If you're walking in this woman's figurative shoes right now, that deep pit in your gut is the emotion that wallpapers the gutter.

Humiliated and broken, she lay there. The religious ones began to cast their words of accusation toward her as she lay at Jesus feet. If ever there was a gutter, this was it. Many Christians today (sometimes myself) would freak out if they were just walking down the street and someone laid a near naked prostitute at their feet. But not Jesus. He knew that true ministry usually isn't what it looks like on the outside, and that it usually isn't packaged in a pretty little box.

The leader of the mob asked Jesus what He was going to do, even going so far as to point out to Jesus what the Mosaic law said about adultery. Plain and simple, she deserved death. Of course, this mob of religious ones wasn't really trying to get this woman killed—they were just trying to use her to trap Jesus in the gutter as a sympathizer of the seductress. They even quoted the law to back up their argument, a practice that finds its modern equivalent every time someone quotes a passage of Scripture only when it suits his needs. But Jesus was the master of silencing His accusers simply by stating truth. And that truth can transform a life being lived in the gutter into a life of rescuing others from the gutter.

Reading this passage, I always ponder what was going on in her head right then. She fully knew that according to Jewish law, death was inevitable. She probably figured this was the end—that the last things she'd embrace would be cold, heavy stones. She had to be wondering where the man was. The one she'd been with only moments before, I mean. Why wasn't he out there going through the same impromptu trial? I'm convinced thoughts like these raced through her mind as she tried to sort out what she knew. But what she did not know was that the Giver of grace was right there with her in the gutter.

Contemplating her situation and their accusations, Jesus paused. Then He stooped down and started writing with His finger in the ground. They kept up with the accusations, and Jesus kept up with the writing. He knew what this was all about—He knew this had nothing to do with the woman and everything to do with Him. So after standing up, He overlooked their attempt to trip Him up and cut to the heart of the matter: "If any one of you is without sin, let him be the first to throw a stone at her."

And then He got back down on the ground and started writing again. What did He write? What were the words that stopped a mob in its tracks? Many Bible scholars have offered their explanations of what He wrote, and while we won't know for sure until we reach heaven, I have my own idea of what it was.

If I were a religious one, an accusation-caster who couldn't wait to start throwing stones, what words would've silenced my accusations? Well, I'd sure want people to think I'm a good person; otherwise my accusations mean nothing. Suppose Jesus was about to expose my imperfections? Maybe, stooped down in that sandy gutter, Jesus started writing out the hidden sins of this woman's accusers. Maybe He wrote that Mr. Smith has an issue with anger, lust, deception, perversion, or something different altogether. Maybe Jesus thought, "Okay, buddy—you want to get sin into the open, I can get sin into the open. Instead of this woman, let's talk about *you* for a second here." If I were Mr. Smith and I saw my depravity in the dirt, I would quietly slip away, embarrassed.

(A few side notes: Why do we so often take pleasure in the spiritual train wrecks that derail in the gutter? And why do we not only ignore those people, but also the gutters they're in? Are we afraid that they're so dirty it'll eventually rub off on us? Or worse, do we lack the compassion to have an effective impact on them? In my experience, it's the latter more than the former.)

The religious ones stood there, stones at the ready, reflecting on the stooping Savior. The Bible says that one by one, from the oldest to the youngest, these men dropped their rocks back onto the sand and walked away in silence, most likely furious that Jesus was able to evade their charges and aid this sinful woman at the same time.

The woman covered her body; Jesus covered her past. Jesus finished His dirt-length novel and stood up to address the woman. As He spoke, He shifted from answering questions to asking them.

"Woman, where are they? Has no one condemned you?" He asked rhetorically. I love this about Jesus—He obviously knew what had gone on, but He wanted to welcome this woman into the conversation, so He asked her a question to which He already knew the answer. I wonder exactly what she was thinking when she said, "No one, sir." No doubt her mind was racing trying, to comprehend everything that had just happened.

"Then neither do I condemn you. Go now and leave your life of sin."

Never before had a gutter produced such an insightful one-way conversation. Jesus asked a pair of questions and then followed them up with two statements. These three elements are the key to understanding the God who embraced the gutter. Let's take an in-depth look at them.

## 1. Woman, where are they? Has no one condemned you?

Jesus did not call this woman by name when He asked this question, because He wasn't *really* asking. I doubt He was so absorbed in what He was writing that He didn't see all the religious ones walking away; He knew where they were, and He knew they'd condemned her to death. I believe He used these questions to let her know He was there to defend her. He was taking up her case.

The God who embraces the gutter is the God who defends the people who dwell there. As He wraps His arms around the hurting, broken, and dejected, those in opposition have to leave. The accusers couldn't carry on with their accusations, and they certainly couldn't have carried out the punishment—they would only have exposed their own mess. Their own pride, arrogance, and fear of exposure sent them running.

Jesus' questions stressed the point that He is capable of defending the ones who are in need.

**2. Neither do I condemn you.**

This bold statement was enough to send the Son of God to the cross. In not condemning this sin, He was essentially forgiving her of it, an exclamation point on His powered position. Jesus had told the accusers that the first person without sin should start throwing the stones, but out of everyone there, *He* was the *only* one without sin, and He wasn't messing around in the dirt trying to find a stone to throw. Instead, He let her know she was safe and that He wasn't going to carry out the punishment she deserved.

For this woman, having a man talk to her and offer her hope, having a man stand before her and embrace her in the gutter—this occurrence was nothing short of a miracle. Jesus stood there and, with His lack of condemnation, released her from her sins, pointing her to the path to get back on track with her destiny. In the midst of her depravity and destruction, Jesus knew the only thing that could restore a derailed destiny was forgiveness. He relieved her from the guilt of her past.

**3. Go now and leave your life of sin.**

Jesus followed forgiveness with a command for action. Action that would propel her in her new life. Go! Leave! Move on! With this little phrase, Jesus was giving her a way out, an invitation to escape the gutter. Jesus could have left her where she was—He'd already gotten her out of her punishment and allowed her to live. He could've left it at the "Neither do I condemn you" part, but He didn't. He embraced her in her gutter, but He refused to let her linger there. He was proactive.

And through that proactive attitude, Jesus is encouraging you and me to get in the gutter for the specific purpose of helping its residents find a new address. A heavenly one. But when we go, we must go in the same way Jesus went, with a "Neither do we condemn you" heart. Because the only way gutter-dwellers will consider leaving the gutter is if we offer them a better alternative through our embrace. We embrace them as a person whom God created and loves instead of judging their actions, and by doing so, we encourage them to leave the gutter, to move on, to "go."

This woman must have been overwhelmed as her mind attempted to process all that had just happened. But Jesus closed the conversation with a simple exhortation: "Leave your life of sin." Simple as that. Essentially, He was saying, "Go on, get out of here and leave your sin in the gutter where it belongs." He offered her an alternative, and we have to assume, though the Bible doesn't specifically say it, that she accepted Jesus' instruction.

The command to leave behind her sin is the truest form of mercy and the most pure definition of grace. Jesus extended grace to her and, in the process, gave her the encouragement and alternative she needed to leave the gutter behind and fulfill her destiny.

Unfortunately, when Christians gather and their tongues start wagging, grace isn't usually the first thing that comes out of their mouths if the conversation turns to someone's mistakes. Many times, the religious ones of the Church are afraid that by offering grace, they're giving the "sinner" a free license to remain in sinful behavior. But we've all been recipients of grace, whether we admit it or not, and most of us have managed to use it responsibly because we are truly repentant.

The Apostle Paul addressed this same topic through the lens of someone who'd been salvaged from the overly righteous gutter. Having been a very good Jew all his life, Paul knew how to condemn with the best of them. In fact, he'd been to many stonings before he came to Christ, so if he'd been around when this woman was caught in adultery, he probably would've been right there with the accusers, ready to help administer punishment. Paul knew a thing or two about grace too—both how to receive it and how to give it, and in the first couple of verses of Romans 6, he addresses the "grace as a license to sin" issue. Here's my paraphrase: "Shall we use this grace as a license to sin? Of course not!" Doesn't get any clearer than that. Is it possible that when true grace is extended, holiness, not debauchery, increases? Yes!

Jesus first embraced this woman in the gutter with loving mercy and grace, then instructed her to go and leave her sinful life. He was saying, "Don't let this area hold you back." Think with her in empathy. Let's say you'd been caught in an action that, by law, called for death. But instead of the electric chair, you were given an immediate reprieve and the freedom to go about your business. More than likely, sin would be the last thing on your mind. I guarantee this woman did not go back to the man she'd been sleeping with and say, "Whew, that was a close one! Now where were we?"

No, the woman caught in adultery escaped the grips of the religious ones and found herself in the arms of a God who embraced the gutter, and when He gave her the instruction not to sin anymore, the last thing she wanted was the warm body of a one-night stand. Instead, she was like anyone else who has benefited from a life-giving act of grace: she had to have walked away wanting to be free. Can't you hear her voice recovering from humiliation? "Jesus, I never want to let You down ..."

We must embrace gutter residents with the same passion Jesus did. We *must* exhibit the same level and type of compassion as Him. Our eyes must see what He sees.

Andy Stanley, the pastor of North Point Community Church in Alpharetta, Ga., co-authored a book for parents and teens with author Stuart Hall, called *The Seven Checkpoints: Seven Principles Every Teenager Needs to Know*. In it, he and Hall address the need to have a heart after God. Stanley stated the obvious, but profound: "If you see what God sees, you'll do what God says."

It's essential. Profound. Elementary. Simple. Do what God says.

What was Jesus' motivation behind this gutter experience? That question is best answered by looking into His biography in the Bible where the chief theme is: people returning to a relationship with their God. God's ultimate plan for each of us is the same—to return to our relationship with Him, and then help others return to *their* relationship with God. The plan may appear in a different package, but ultimately, we are to fulfill our role in the restoration process.

Our lives, including every interaction we have with pre-Christians, are to be used to move people back to God if they aren't in a relationship with Him, or closer to Him if they are. Consider the words Paul chose when instructing a young Timothy: "But you, keep your head in all situations, endure hardship, do the work of an evangelist, discharge all the duties of your ministry" (2 Tim. 4:5).

Now, when Paul is telling Timothy that doing the work of an evangelist is one of the duties of the ministry, he isn't saying that every Christian needs to have his own television ministry supported by "ministry partners." That is not an evangelist. He isn't saying everyone should leave their jobs and go on the preaching circuit. That is not an evangelist either. I read "evangelist" in this verse to mean people who are consumed with the singular message of the saving power of Jesus. People who are deliberate in their motivations, and who allow every part of their lives to be used to communicate the hope that lies in Jesus and His cross.

Many times we dodge spiritual conversations or fuss about spiritual environments that may include pre-Christian people. We have a bad taste because of a past experience we have had with an "evangelist" or someone else preaching the "good news." Remember Pastor Bible? He would consider himself an evangelist, but after I approached him to discuss his beliefs, he scolded me.

Words cannot express the embarrassment I felt as this man called people "faggots" and "whores," or as he told everyone within earshot that they "will all burn in hell." Here's a guy who claims to bring the same Gospel as me, but he's going about it the exact wrong way, pronouncing judgment and a death sentence to everyone. When I finally was able to get a word in and ask him why he was there, he responded with a quick, "Everyone here is going to hell!"

The irony? He later said he "had the Good News." Really?

The crowd grew tired of this man's anger and "righteous" threats, and they began to disperse. Maybe, like me, their ears were ringing from his rant. As I walked away, the piercing rasp of his voice played over and over in my mind. "I am an evangelist for Jesus with the Good News. I am an evangelist for Jesus with the Good News."

From a spiritual standpoint, the gutter is the place where people without Christ have been abandoned to the world and its ways. Dejected, broken, and many times discouraged to the point of giving up, most people in the gutter know their lives are empty. To have someone invade their environment with a screaming, violent, and hostile tirade is not Christlike; if anything, it is anti-Christlike.

Just stroll through the Gospels. Read through Matthew, Mark, Luke … and see what John wrote about how Jesus reacted and responded to those in the gutter. I did it and came away surprised. As I looked for patterns and examples to follow, I noticed how Jesus embraced the gutter instead of condemning it. When Jesus faced someone imprisoned by the gutter, someone whose heart was aware of its depravity, someone who was hurting, dejected, and discouraged, He spoke a message of hope, grace, and mercy. He confronted them with comfort in His redeeming and faithful love.

When Jesus came across the self-proclaimed righteous and judgmental, He confronted them as well, but not with grace and mercy. For this crowd, Jesus came with the power of the law. He called them snakes. A "brood of vipers," to be exact (Matt. 3:7, 12:34, 23:33). He called them dead on the inside, or "whitewashed tombs" (Matt. 23:27).

He judged those who judged and loved those who needed love.

There were only two central themes in the messages Jesus taught. To the hardened ones who dwelt in the high towers of religious routine, He gave them the law. To the unchurched, pre-Christian, seekers, He gave eternal hope. I noticed something as I was stung by these Gospel examples, stunned by the simplicity of it all and the way these two themes tie in with God's kingdom: Whatever you sow, you'll reap; what you give is what you get. Said another way, the tool you use on other people will be the same tool applied to your life.

For the screaming preacher dispatching verbal abrasions, I am fearful.

When I reflect on what we are trying to accomplish with XXXchurch, I seek hope. I am uncomfortable with titles, but okay with descriptions, so even though my upbringing in the Christian ghetto has taught me to detest the term, I am an "evangelist" in its purest biblical sense. Not according to the world, but to the Word. I exist to do what Paul said: to discharge (another translation says "fulfill") my ministry and do the work of a soul winner. I want to leverage my life so that the God who chose to send His Son through the gutter can finally embrace His children who are lost in the gutter.

What will my life be worth if I don't do what He has asked me to do? What will my life be if I look at a gutter-dweller's pain and despair and do nothing to help him come to know Christ? If we have the eyesight to see people the way God does, it becomes impossible to not embrace them. It is impossible not to embrace the gutter.

To those willing and wanting to live life to its fullest, the gutter becomes a viable option. Add to that the fact that some incredible people have once lived there.

You. Me. Us.

Jesus.

We *are* the gutter, and Jesus still embraces us wholeheartedly. We have all been there, and now we need to go back there—with different vision.

Consider the past. You were there.

Consider the present. You can make a difference in the gutter.

Consider the future. You must help sustain an ongoing effort to the gutter. As Christians, we can't merely go to the gutter to embrace it or fulfill it just for today. We need to go to fulfill the kingdom. The rewards are too great not to.

# 08

# THE ULTIMATE GUTTER

## CHAPTER EIGHT

The gutter can be lonely. And when you look at it from a spiritual sense in today's society, it seems like more people live *in* the gutter than *out*. The gutter is also a self-imposed place of separation from that which God has destined for you, and when I look around, I see a lot of people whose lives are just like that.

Those in the gutter often feel left out. Alone. Abandoned. Abused. But these feelings, while real, aren't necessarily accurate. God is always with us, even when we don't feel like He is. Only Jesus has known the complete abandonment of a God whose face is turned away. In His role as Savior, Jesus took on the ultimate punishment—abandonment from God—and He let everyone know how horrible it was in Matthew 27:46: "Jesus cried out in a loud voice, 'Eloi, Eloi, lama sabachthani?'—which means, 'My God, my God, why have you forsaken me?'"

Think about it. Here's a man whose body had gone beyond the limits of normal suffering, a man who was about to die and whose strength had nearly ebbed completely away. But in that moment of weakness and frailty, blood flowing everywhere, pain wracking every cubic inch of His body, the only time we're told He cried with a "loud voice" was when God forsook Him. That's pain.

The last earthly gutter Jesus visited in human form was located in the hills on the outskirts of Jerusalem. Resembling a skull, the hill Golgotha was a place where the forgotten were left to die, surrounded by garbage deposited by those who lived in the city. It wasn't fancy, it wasn't clean, it wasn't populated—it was filthy and isolated, the ultimate gutter. But out of this gutter rose a gnarled wooden image of redemption that salvaged mankind and reconciled them to God.

Walking through a local mall recently, I noticed the number of crosses that are now being worn as jewelry. Necks and ears decked out with the tool that killed Jesus. Upon the zillionth sighting I began to wonder if any of these people really *understood* what they were wearing. I didn't blame them, and I wasn't upset at their choice of jewelry, but I did realize that it's easier to wear gold on your neck than wood on your back. (Please don't anyone make that into a Christian T-shirt. Thank you.) I stopped walking and reflected.

Can you imagine the scene when Jesus was sent to die? Probably just about everyone on the planet has seen *The Passion of the Christ* by now, but before I had watched it, I'd never really been able to gain a clear picture of the crucifixion. I lacked so much understanding of what really occurred. As a speaker, I've talked about the cross hundreds of times, but I don't really think I ever got it until I saw that movie, because the pictures on the screen say it better than words ever could.

As the King of the Universe died a cruel death, mankind was rescued from the gutter. As onlookers perceived physical darkness, a brilliant light of Hope was revealed. The daytime sky grew dark and became a silhouette for the backdrop of salvation. The eerie scene settled over the disciples in the gutter of Golgotha.

The Ultimate Gutter was beautiful and cruel, and as I watched the film's depiction of the final moments of the crucifixion, I saw my emotions perfectly illustrated. In the middle of Golgotha's hillside, Jesus gave up His life for a brutal, awful death on the cross. This particular means of execution was essentially a way to torture people to death, and found its roots in the ancient Assyrians, who were the first to crucify criminals by impaling them on a stake. The Romans refined the process and began to nail them to a cross, and the tormented usually spent several days waiting for death to overtake them.

It was absolute torture, and until I saw *The Passion*, my mind's eye had never really grasped it, even though the Bible described each of the elements Jesus willingly endured so the gutter could be a place of Hope:

- The Bible says Jesus was scourged (Matt. 27:26).
- The Bible says He was beaten (Luke 22:63-64).
- The Bible says He was humiliated and spit upon (Matt. 27:30).
- The Bible says He was tortured, and His beard was plucked from His face (Isa. 50:6).
- The Bible says He was mocked (Matt. 27:26-29).
- The Bible says He was stripped naked (Matt. 27:35).
- The Bible says He was nailed to the cross (Matt. 27:38; John 20:25).

Scripture could not paint a more darkened picture, but I'd always seen it in metaphorical terms. The darkness was a reference to the gutter. Consider the words of 1 Samuel 2:9-10: "He will guard the feet of his saints, but *the wicked will be silenced in darkness*. It is not by strength that one prevails" (emphasis added).

In other words, as a created being, Satan thought his nemesis Jesus had failed at the cross. In fact, the cross was only the beginning of the victory, and Satan was silenced as Jesus died there.

Through physical strength, Jesus could have tried to resist the power of death's tug, but He didn't take that route. Instead, He prevailed through spiritual strength, enduring the pain and shame to the point of willingly giving His hands to be nailed. He willingly gave His forehead to bear its thorny crown. He willingly gave His side to be gouged. He willingly gave His feet to be riveted. Wickedness and the luring deceit of the gutter lost while Jesus prevailed. I prevailed. You prevailed.

Many argue that no man could have endured what Jesus faced and made it all the way to the cross. Based on that assumption, the standard skeptic asserts that the entire Calvary scene has been embellished somehow. This notion became the context and framework of a conversation I had with Jimmy D., the porn producer. Remember him? Standing outside a coffee house on Sunset Boulevard, Jimmy and I talked about *The Passion of the Christ*. Because he has filmmaking knowledge, he likes to critique movies, so he began to describe what he would have done differently in the production. I stood and listened to him alternately compliment and condemn the movie's artistic value.

But it was his final commentary that grabbed me. In so many words, Jimmy said there is no man alive who could have endured so much torture, and that he felt Mel Gibson had tried to exploit the viewer with this violent and graphic depiction of death. (I suppressed a chuckle, finding it a tad ironic that a pornographer was complaining about a movie being too graphic and made in order to exploit the viewer.) Jimmy continued, standing firm on his belief that any man alive would have died at the scourging, long before the cross was introduced. He didn't have to say anymore. Since he knew my background and faith, Jimmy stopped a few words shy of saying what so many skeptics state to me as their final argument in a Jesus conversation: that a man could not have endured the torture as long as Jesus did.

Any eavesdropping Christian would have been frustrated that I didn't quickly jump in and defend the cross. First off, the cross defends itself. But beyond that, I wanted Jimmy to keep talking, because he was building a great case for belief in Jesus' deity. The finality of his position was that mortal man could not have endured. And to that I said, "Jimmy, you're absolutely right. Mortal man would have died hours before Jesus willingly did. But that's just all the more power that Jesus had, because He was not mortal man. He was God. Man did not endure the torture, Jesus did." Man's strength, like Jimmy asserted, would have died. But Jimmy didn't connect the final dots—that Jesus' all-powerful nature is what destroyed the darkness.

In Romans, Paul lays out the foundations of the road to Calvary and why it is our only hope to escape life's mistakes. Five verses spell out the stepping stones we can use to understand God's final plan, starting in Romans 3:23: "For all have sinned and fall short of the glory of God." Everyone makes mistakes and misses God's mark for success in life. We fall short, and that fall ultimately puts us in the emotional, physical, and spiritual gutter.

Because of missing the mark, man and God are separated. Because of the mistakes we make (i.e., sin) we are separated from the holy and perfect God. But we don't have to stay that way, according to the next stepping stone, Romans 5:8: "But God demonstrates his own love for us in this: While we were still sinners, Christ died for us." While we were still missing the mark, in the middle of our mess, God expressed His desire to be reunited to us, a desire that took human form in the man of Jesus. In a sense, Jesus went to the gutter specifically to get us out of it. He even said so Himself when He told the disciples nobody could ever get to God, escaping the gutter, unless they go through Him (John 14:6). After all, Jesus is the only one who ever conquered it.

Paul must have been addressing the book of Romans to a bunch of skeptics, because he fires off the reason why sins and mistakes must be accounted for in chapter 6, verse 23: "For the wages of sin is death, but the gift of God is eternal life in Christ Jesus our Lord." The results of a life in sin: Death. Yes, death! The sure way to die is to live in the gutter, in total separation from God. Many say, "Come on, a physical death? Please!" But I'm more concerned about a spiritual death than a physical death, since Jesus told us not to worry about what will happen to our physical body, but to take care of our spiritual lives first (Matt. 6:25-34).

When Jesus hung on the cross, He did so desiring that every person would accept His free gift of life. The only qualifier is that you believe in Him, and I'm not talking about a belief of existence here, either—even demons believe that. I'm talking about a belief in the values, standards, and purpose of confessing that Jesus Christ is who He said He is and will do what He said He would do. It's a belief that's so strong, you aren't afraid to articulate it, which is exactly what the next stepping stone calls for. Romans 10:9 says, that if "you confess with your mouth, 'Jesus is Lord,' and believe in your heart that God raised him from the dead, you will be saved." Four verses later, the Bible says the same thing: "Everyone who calls on the name of the Lord will be saved."

See, people make it harder than it really is. Jesus made it simple; Calvary made it complete. At Calvary, mankind discovered that its own life's mess is nothing more than a short-term pleasure that ends in darkness and death. Regardless of how strong someone thinks he is, only Jesus can rescue from the all-consuming gutter. He is the *only* answer for gutter dwellers.

Without Jesus, our situation is bleak. Many people find themselves in the gutter and ask, "How did I get here?" And while that's an important question, the *more* important question is, "How will I get out?" Here's the answer to the first question: All of humanity, you and me included, followed our own desires and found ourselves in need of a Savior. We were in a bind, in need of rescue. Roy Lessin, an author of inspirational writings, poetically described our need this way: "If our greatest need had been information, God would have sent an educator. If our greatest need had been technology, God would have sent us a scientist. If our greatest need had been money, God would have sent us an economist. But since our greatest need was forgiveness, God sent us a Savior."[1]

I can't begin to understand what it must take to willingly die for someone you love, much less for someone you know may reject the act of love. But had Jesus not done so, I would still be separated from God and doomed to a destiny of death.

"For Christ died for sins once for all, the righteous for the unrighteous, to bring you to God" (1 Pet. 3:18a).

So that I could be brought to God ...

The essential meaning of the cross is this: Jesus took my place. In 1 Peter 2:24 we read, "He himself bore our sins in his body on the tree, so that we might die to sins and live for righteousness; by his wounds you have been healed."

Zondervan offers the following from its Starting Point Study Bible:

> The cross reveals our need for a Savior. When a criminal faces the penalty imposed by law, he or she comes to understand the severity of his or her actions. When we see Jesus at the cross—when we witness the agony, pain, shame, and death He suffered—we can understand how offensive our sins are in the eyes of a holy God. The prophet Isaiah foresaw the Messiah's

---

1. Accessed at *www.sermons.org/christmas5.html*.

suffering: "Surely he took up our infirmities and carried our
sorrows ... But he was pierced for our transgressions, he was
crushed for our iniquities" (Isa. 53:4-5).

Back to the movie, *The Passion of the Christ*. When I left the theater, I
felt like I had just been slugged in the stomach. It was an intense story
told with vivid detail and astonishingly beautiful imagery, but even as I
departed, I realized I'd just experienced a firsthand look at the gutter.

In case you lived in a cave for the entire two years before the movie
came out and therefore don't know this, I'll fill you in. Mel Gibson, the
man behind the camera, underwent a firestorm of negativity for even
attempting the movie. He tried to paint a picture of the gutter, and many
in the secular arena cursed him for making such a "violent depiction."
Never mind that hundreds of horror movies were produced prior to this
with little fanfare or worry over their violent content, but show the gutter
and its effects and you have a fight on your hands. People don't like to
think about, much less see, Jesus being beaten down in the gutter.

Many people hated the fact that *The Passion* even existed, and all it did
was illustrate the gutter. Jesus, through the cross, was made accessible
to every man. The cross overcame the acts that sent us into separation
from God when Adam and Eve disobediently ate from the one fruit
tree, dooming the rest of mankind. Before the fruit from the tree of the
knowledge of good and evil had touched man's lips, mankind had never
known the gutter, because the gutter didn't exist. But the moment Adam
and Eve ate the fruit, the gutter of wrong choices, disobedience, pain,
perversion, and misguided intent was created. Motive and agenda were
created. But thousands of years later as Jesus was abandoned and left for
dead, God gave humankind the ability to get out of the gutter.

Through one tree, mankind collided with the gutter. Through another,
mankind was delivered from the effects of the gutter.

So if Jesus rescued me from the gutter, why must I get in the gutter? Shouldn't this mean I never have to come in contact with the gutter again? NO! The opposite is true. Since I've been rescued from the gutter, I can now go back and show other people the way out, too. Through the cross, I have been given a mandate to serve, love, and embrace those who have yet to find freedom in Jesus.

Jesus hung alone, suspended between heaven and earth. With infinite power, He reached up and grasped the hand of God while reaching down to clasp the hand of a gutter-lodged people. He pulled God down a little. He pulled us up a little. Finally, through Jesus, God and mankind were on equal ground. Jesus joined our hands and cried out, "It is finished!"

Simply put, gutter living was finished at the cross. No longer could a person's existence be defined by where he or she had been. My past ... your past ... their past ... all were eliminated by the provision of the cross. In its simplest definition, the cross was the sweet-smelling rose that surfaced into sight from out of the gutter.

In the midst of the garbage heap hung Jesus, the Son of God. The most priceless creation of all time went to the ultimate gutter to eliminate the effects of that gutter. He went there so humankind no longer has to be imprisoned there. You and I now have the freedom to live a life of freedom in Him.

His life began in the gutter and it ended there. That alone should clearly illustrate His commitment to the people in it. They—we—are His family.

# YOUR GUTTER

**SECTION THREE**

# 09
# STRANGERS IN THE GUTTER

## CHAPTER NINE

I hope by now you've at least begun to see the need for us to go to the gutter, and maybe you're starting to think, "Yeah, this sounds great and all, but I don't really know where to go." So many times we think we have to go far away to get in the gutter, but really—there's a gutter in your backyard. As Christians, we ought to have relationships with the people in our communities, with our neighbors, with everyone we meet.

Or maybe you're in the professional ministry, a youth pastor or pastor or traveling evangelist, and you're wondering how you can go to the gutter. For most of you, I'd say, "Keep it up." Keep up what you're doing, but make sure you're doing it for the right reasons. If you're a youth pastor, are you honestly, earnestly trying to make a difference in the lives of your students and their pre-Christian friends, or are you just playing babysitter? If you're a senior pastor, do you see what God sees or only what the board of elders tells you to see? If you're in the traveling ministry, do you take Christ with you at all times, or only when you get on stage? Getting in the gutter is a lifestyle of consistently and constantly perceiving the world through God's eyes.

If the idea of getting in the gutter sounds good to you, but still a little daunting, let me offer you some encouragement—you are not accepting this mission alone. God has not called you to win the entire world by yourself. The rest of this chapter is full of stories of ordinary people just like you who have obeyed God's call on their lives, gone to the gutter, and succeeded. Every story is different, and though their methods often vary, the people I mention in the next few chapters are all people just like you. Their talents differ, but they all have a heart for the gutter. It is my prayer that as you read about their hearts for the gutter, you will develop one of your own.

## YWAM AMSTERDAM

I've metaphorically referred to the gutter as the Red Light District a few times in this book, but a few years ago I found myself smack in the middle of the real thing. Yep, *the* Red Light District. I'd gone to Amsterdam to visit the folks at YWAM Amsterdam and to see some of the ministry they were doing there, and I have to say I was pretty surprised at what I found.

First of all, the Red Light District is just plain crazy. There's really no other way to describe it. Think of a sin, any sin. Got it? It's probably legal there: prostitution, pornography, "interactive" sex shows, "soft" drugs— the works. And the city itself is unashamed of this part of town; it's a regular tourist attraction boasted about as something "you have to check out for yourself" on the city's website. One of the most ironic things about the Red Light District is the Oude Kerk, a fourteenth-century cathedral located in the middle of the district. It's a church in building only, however—open to the public for tours and such, but there is no ministry coming from within its walls.

Where the Oude Kerk is *not* bringing Christ's light into the Red Light District, The Cleft is. The Cleft is the primary arm of YWAM Amsterdam's reach into the Red Light District. In 1979, they started renting out an old hotel, dedicating it to evangelism outreaches to the district. Since that time, The Cleft has become a place of refuge to the marginalized people of the Red Light District, establishing a sense of family for the homeless, the drug addicts, the prostitutes, or other people who feel like they don't belong. It's become so much of a hope that the staff refers to it as "The Promised Land."

YWAM Amsterdam has a variety of ministries, like "De Poort" (Dutch for "The Gateway"), a learning institution specifically dedicated to training Christians to reach the urban world. They also have a youth hangout called "Sam's Inn" (short for "Samaritan's Inn") that houses YWAM offices, a café, a music shop, a recording studio, and other stuff they use to reach into the community.

The Cleft is a true exploration of the gutter, a guidepost to the lost, continually available to show them the way out. See, they don't just stand on the corner and preach at the passersby. No, since they're in the midst of one of the most sinful places on earth, they have to be creative and innovative in their methods, using their minds essentially to outsmart the enemy. They have to work hard to spread the love of Jesus, which they do through practical means and by simply establishing relationships with the people who surround them.

They have evening services where they explain the Gospel in short and easy ways, using speakers, film, drama, and testimonies from people who've been rescued from the gutter. In the afternoons, the building opens to the general public, and the staff provides reading material, games, and refreshments like tea and coffee or sandwiches and soup. They hand out clothes to those who need them. They sit and chat with those who desire a listening ear. Basically, they just use the time to hang out in the gutter, building relationships with gutter-dwellers in the hopes of helping them out.

Is it easy? No. Is it worth it? Absolutely. And what I really love about the whole thing is that while they have this thriving ministry at The Cleft, they don't stay there. They take the Gospel into the streets, going to the prostitutes and building relationships with them, inviting them to The Cleft for a warm meal or a chat. Most of the prostitutes in the city are drug addicts, so YWAM's team tries to help them out of *that* gutter, visiting them in rehab centers, hospitals, or even prison.

In the Red Light District, the prostitutes solicit business by standing in windows, to make themselves look as attractive as they can. The YWAM workers even try to influence these women, taking them coffee and tea, organizing fun events they can attend, or just simply celebrating their birthdays. Their whole motivation is to establish a relationship in order to let the light of Christ shine into that dark, dark place. It's working.

And they're still coming up with ideas. Now they're trying to launch a ministry to homosexuals and another ministry to the children growing up in the Red Light District. This is the type of passion and fervor that comes from a gutter-focused lifestyle—it's a passion that forces you to be creative and smart, to come to gutter-dwellers on their terms in order to find success. They are living out Matthew 10:16, where Jesus said, "I am sending you out like sheep among wolves. Therefore be as shrewd as snakes and as innocent as doves."

Shrewdness and innocence are necessities for the gutter.

## MY FRIEND HARVEY

Harvey Carey was born and raised in the hard part of Chicago. Living in the heart of the city, he saw his fair share of poverty, crime, drugs, and the like while growing up, but despite his surroundings and the low expectations they engendered, he focused on his education (thanks largely to his mother) and graduated with honors from high school, moving on from there to college where he had his first encounter with Jesus.

After his conversion, God called Harvey into full-time ministry, so he went to seminary in Dallas, and while he was there, the Lord strongly impressed upon him the desire to go to Detroit to start a church that would be called "Citadel." He didn't know exactly what to do with it, so he put it at the back of his mind, married a sweet girl, became a youth pastor in Chicago, and began to climb the ranks to associate pastor.

His ministry in Chicago thrived, but Harvey never forgot God's call to Detroit. He began to seek out an opportunity to get to the Motor City and eventually, through the cooperation of a local church there, planted Citadel of Faith Covenant Church in the poorest ZIP code in the state of Michigan—right in the heart of Detroit. He was essentially back in the gutter in which he'd been raised.

In only their first year there, Harvey and his family saw amazing results as they reached out to their community. They hosted the area's largest "Back to School" rally, giving away school supplies, book bags, gift certificates for uniforms, and tons more, all free for the community. They established a tutorial program for area third graders; they hosted home ownership and health empowerment forums; and in the summers, they started having movie nights every Friday. They reach out to the gutter, working to stay innovative and practical in their approach.

But my favorite story of Harvey in Detroit is how he pretty much closed down a crack house single-handedly, just by obeying God and by going to the gutter. When he first got to the city, someone told him about a crack house that was in operation near a park where the neighborhood children played. He made it his personal mission, his "job," if you will, to go there every day and get to know the drug dealers.

Of course, his actions raised a few eyebrows of concern, but he felt a personal conviction that he was supposed to be doing it, so he did. He would go in the morning and stay until late in the evening, just hanging out with drug dealers, finding out about them, talking to them. Day after day, he'd head into the gutter. And whenever a car would pull up to pick up drugs, he would start witnessing to those people before the dealer could make an offer, usually finding that the prospective buyers weren't really ready to hear anything about Jesus. They would screech away—no sale.

Then he got his church involved, holding prayer meetings in front of the crack house on its busiest nights. Basically, they just got on the level of the gutter—and it worked. Now that crack house is no longer in business. The park is safe; the neighborhood kids are free of that up-close influence; and the Gospel is preached in the gutter.

Here's something I didn't tell you. When the crack house by the park closed down, it reopened at a different location. Guess who was there to meet the dealers? When it closed down and relocated again, Harvey and the Citadel family found out the new location and showed back up. Through three relocations in all, this crack house and these dealers could not escape the love of Jesus in the person of Harvey. That is serious love for the gutter.

Harvey's rationale for all this? God called him to start a church in the inner-city gutter of Detroit, and the call was strong—and Harvey's burden deep. His ultimate goal: When people think of Detroit, he wants them to think "church." Though it's a noble and audacious goal, Harvey knows that if the Church at large is ever going to grow to that point, it must reach into the gutter with the love of Christ. Jesus hung out with tax collectors and the like, but most pastors and spiritual leaders today only hang around other religious people—Pharisees and scribes. Harvey would rather model himself after Jesus and go where He went. To the gutter.

## MY FRIEND DAVE

Mention the word "gutter" to Dave, and he'll tell you it means he has to move his car off the street on Tuesday and Wednesday or he'll get a ticket from the street sweeper. Apparently the gutters get pretty dirty there in Laguna Beach, California. But that's just about it when it comes to surface dirt it isn't even close to being an outward gutter like Amsterdam or inner-city Detroit; it's quite the opposite.

Dave describes Laguna Beach as the most SUV-driving, Starbucks-drinking, silicone-implanted, twenty-four-hour-fitness, low-carb, who-has-the-most-toys, surface-level, non-engaging, suburban place on earth. But it's also a gutter—a gutter of self. A gutter Dave dives into whenever he isn't on the road.

See, Dave is the singer for the band PAX217, so he sees a lot of different gutters in his travels, and he loves to step into them to see what makes people tick. He's fascinated by how people arrive at their belief systems. He loves to find out why and what they love, hate, respect, and cherish, and he's motivated to stay in the gutter because he knows a universal truth about it: If a Christian doesn't get in the gutter, he doesn't get challenged. And when he doesn't get challenged (and a little bit uncomfortable), he gets apathetic and bored.

Dave's seen a lot of gutters, but he's most familiar with his hometown of

Laguna Beach and its airs of success. But it's all a façade, a big show to hide the desperation for fulfillment that lies underneath, a fulfillment that will never occur outside of God's will.

The thing I love about Dave is how aware he is of the different gutters of the world and all the different people who are dwelling there. When I hang out with Dave, I see an enormous, genuine love for people that, sadly, I don't see in a lot of other Christians, including myself. We'll walk into a Starbucks or some restaurant, and the menu is usually the last thing Dave looks for. He notices the people.

I remember a time when we saw a man reading the Bible while drinking his coffee. Dave approached the man, not caring that he might be interrupting his Bible study; he wanted to find out what the man was reading and what God was putting on his heart today. I couldn't tell if the man was a Christian or just someone checking out the book. You see, I didn't know because I didn't stop and have time for that guy. I was too busy ordering some coffee for a long trip we were about to make home.

Coffee ready, I grabbed Dave in the midst of their conversation and told him we had to go. "Go where?" Dave replied. What was so important that we had to leave right then and there? Why couldn't he stay and talk with this guy? Of course, I had to get home, so Dave cut the conversation short, but I'll never forget the attitude he had about it. This guy was the most important thing to him right then. Believe me, next time I go into Starbucks, my eyes aren't going to be on the menu; I'll have time for the gutter that day.

One morning, early, the phone rang. I picked it up and it was Dave, calling me to tell me what happened to him the night before. He said his wife, Allison, had gone to bed, so he decided to take some photographs of the city at night. Since his camera bag was in the car, he headed over to the alley where the car was parked and began searching for the bag in the trunk. He then heard a young male voice behind him, "Hey, I couldn't help but notice how cute you are. You want to party with me?" Dave had never been hit on by another man, and he was a bit stunned.

"I declined, and found it funny when he drove off kind of irritated," Dave said. But then he began to realize he'd blown a great opportunity to get into the gutter—an open invitation, even. "As I was walking back to my place, I thought to myself, 'What would've happened if I'd said, 'Okay' and gotten in the car with him? What would we have said to each other, how awkward would it have been? Or would it have been awkward at all? Could I have found myself in a bar at 2 a.m. with a complete stranger whom I know had very different beliefs from me? Would I have been able to offer him a love he wasn't expecting? A genuine love of persons, the type of love Christ would have offered?'"

Bold, gutter-defying notions.

Dave continued, "I realized I might have missed an opportunity not just to 'witness,' but to engage a person's life in a way that would have given him hope and a memory of someone who loved him as he was." As he examined his own heart about this encounter with the gutter, he began to realize fear is what kept him out of it that night.

Okay, I can't even imagine coming in at 2 a.m. after hanging out with a guy in a bar all night. What would I say to my wife? How would I explain it? What if I saw people I knew? These questions and a zillion others went through my mind (and they're probably going through yours)—and they're all perfectly legitimate reasons why I would not have done it. I probably would have jokingly told the story to my friends about getting hit on by another man.

Not Dave. He told me the story that next morning, and yes, we laughed, and I gave him a hard time about it. But through it all, I could hear that he genuinely wished he could start that night over again so he could go to the gutter.

I told Dave I was writing this book and asked him to give me his thoughts on the gutter. My intent was to sum them up in a nifty book format, all journalistic-style, but after I read what he had to write, I knew I'd be better off just letting Dave speak for himself.

> I believe many of us have been taught by our 'leaders,' whether that be our families or our Church families, to be afraid of the temptation of what the world has to offer. But why should someone who has different beliefs be my enemy? Shouldn't I refer to them as God's creation? Though they might not have received the gift of Christ, they are still extremely beautiful. It is time that we not be afraid of the unknown or the unrighteous, but rather embrace them as someone like us. The more I remind myself of how much Christ loves me the same on my worst day as He does on my best day, the more I am reminded to get in the gutter and love others.

## MY FRIEND RYAN

Ryan has been an "extreme" (sorry, I meant "X-treme") sort of guy for a while now. He likes to surf, skate, and ride motorcycles. And he's a Christian. A lot of times we're uncomfortable with the gutter because the people there make us uncomfortable. But sometimes it isn't the people— it's the idea of talking about Jesus to these people. We think, *Those people are really hard. God can't save them.*

Okay, maybe we don't think that exactly, but the way we act toward some gutter-dwellers gives that message. The gutter Ryan reaches is made up of hard people like that—skaters and surfers and bikers. He's into all those things, but he didn't try to start up "Christian skaters" or

"Christian bikers" clubs so he could participate in these activities in a "safe" environment. Instead, he just did them and wound up hanging out with a whole bunch of folks who don't know Jesus. Sometimes the gutter is made up of people who look a lot like you.

What's great about Ryan's gutter is that he has opportunities to share the Gospel with these people who no one else would have. Take, for example, the biker wedding he officiated. It wasn't an extremely huge affair, but he laughingly says he was the only one there with a shirt that buttoned. (The happy couple sported matching "West Coast Choppers" T-shirts.) But because of his influence, he was able to preach a great Christian wedding to a captive audience—and be accepted.

Or how about Ryan's friend, Meatball. Meatball is a bike mechanic, and a darn good one—but he's a little dirty. His shop is full of pornography, and he's rough around the edges, but Ryan still takes his bike to Meatball because he sees it as an opportunity to share some of Christ's love with the guy. Boy, does Ryan take heat from some of his Christian friends for it. They don't understand why he goes into this dirty, porn-ridden shop when he can get the same work done on his bike in a cleaner environment. Ryan's answer is simple: "If I don't do it, who will?"

## DRAWING CONCLUSIONS

Four different stories in four different worlds. Four different methods—all of them effective—on reaching the gutter. Let's sum up:

**YWAM Amsterdam:**
Creative. Unique. Bold. Outrageous. They live in the gutter and continually adapt to its complexities.

**Harvey:**
He sees the gutter, and wants to take it over.

**Dave:**
He makes time for the gutter and he tries not to fear it.

**Ryan:**
He finds the gutter all around him because of his interests. He knows it's up to him to do his part.

So what can we learn from all this? Do you see a common thread here? I think it all comes down to one word, really: willingness. In each of these examples, people exhibit a willingness to go into the gutter and do what God has called them to do. A willingness to defy the enemy and step into his realm to rescue people from it.

You'll also notice that these people's gutters are all around them. They don't have to travel far away to some distant land in order to get into the gutter—they find gutter-dwellers at their feet, and like Christ, they stop what they're doing in order to invest some time into the life of a gutter-dweller. They put aside the fear and discomfort that might well up in them when they look at the gutter, and then they go.

They go and they go some more because once you get in the gutter, you find that you want to go back. So what are some gutters around you that you can get involved in? You may not have a Red Light District or crack house or biker garage near you, but I can almost guarantee there's a Starbucks. Or a grocery store. Or a street corner. Or any number of things. Look hard enough and you'll find a gutter you can get in; just look with God's eyes.

In the words of Ryan: If you don't go, who will?

# 10
# THE BACKSTAGE GUTTER

Long ago, in the late '80s when heavy metal music was at its zenith, a band dared to combine the metal sound, a biblical worldview, and a whole lot of yellow and black stuff. Of course, I'm talking about Stryper, *the* biggest Christian metal band ever. If you lived through the '80s and were a "hip" Christian, more than likely you heard some of Stryper's tunes. These guys were everywhere—and they had to deal with a lot of negativity from a lot of Christian leaders because of it.

In interview after interview, these guys would have to defend their music, the way they dressed, their tours, their album covers, their lyrics—just about everything. I used to love the band, and I remember reading an interview with Tim Gaines, the bass player, where he just point-blank came out and said something like, "If you don't like our music, don't listen to it. Don't eat or drink with sinners either."

Perfect. That is a gutter mentality.

The debate over so-called Christian music rages on today. Wherever there is a group of Christians making music that peers into the gutter, there will be another group of Christians saying their music is ungodly. Music is such a huge part of our culture, but it can't reach into the gutter by itself. Yet when musicians try to use it as an avenue to get into the gutter, a naysayer will come along and focus on the avenue instead of on the lost person that avenue is designed to reach.

If we're all supposed to go to the gutter—to the world—then why are so many bands lambasted for crossing over to the mainstream market? Isn't that what we're *all* supposed to be doing?

Sometimes I get really pissed off when I see so-called Christians attacking other Christians for getting into the gutter. Look, if God hasn't called them to a particular gutter, like secular musicians, for example, then by all means they shouldn't go into that gutter. But I think they get confused and determine that since *they* aren't called to that gutter, *no one* is called to that gutter. So instead of getting on board with a gutter-driven band, they tear that band down and generate division about that band's mission.

I found a couple of articles on the Internet that illustrate this point perfectly. The first is about a band called Chevelle, some really cool, authentic guys who have worked hard as musicians and have finally achieved notoriety in mainstream music circles. In 2003, they got invited on the popular Ozzfest tour, where they got a chance to dive daily into the gutter of secular music. It was a great opportunity for them, but as soon as they agreed to do it, here came the naysayers from the Evangel Society:

By touring with Ozzfest, Chevelle could lend tacit support to the other bands on tour. While not saying that they support each individual band they play with, Chevelle also chose not to criticize them, or to express any hesitancy about associating with them. All press reports from the tour indicate that Chevelle interacts with Marilyn Manson in a friendly fashion. Does this action simply show Christian love? Perhaps, but bands are known by the company they keep ...

Fans could easily consider Chevelle's presence at Ozzfest a soft endorsement of the other bands. At a minimum, fans see that Chevelle does not disagree with the other bands enough to make an issue about it. Through being featured as part of the tour, Chevelle supports the promotion and profitability of Ozzfest, lending further unspoken support to these anti-Christian bands ...

Those who delight in blaspheming and mocking Christianity will find it strange that a Christian band takes pride in complacently touring with those who attack their views. Ozzfest is also associated with lifestyles and activities, such as heavy drinking, that many would expect that Christians would prefer not to take part in. Indeed, fans might view Chevelle as trying to fit into the Ozzfest group—to be one of the world—rather than standing up for their Christian beliefs.[1]

Now, I readily admit that the guy who wrote this article sounded like he genuinely believed in Chevelle as a band, and he didn't dive off the deep end like so many Christian critics do, but he still expressed a fair amount of worry, throwing doubt on the band and its "soft endorsement" of non-Christian bands. Never mind that Chevelle has a rare opportunity to exhibit the love of Christ to its secular peers.

---

1. Michael Francisco, "Chevelle at Ozzfest: Confused and Muffled Christianity," July 29, 2003, *www.evangelsociety.org/francisco/chevelle.html.*

Another band tackled by the Evangel Society is Pillar. In an article from July 21, 2003, Keith Miller offers his idea of the proper way a Christian band should cross over to the mainstream market. His guinea pig was Pillar, and I should note that Miller wrote the following at the beginning of his article:

> This article is not attempting to single out Pillar as traitorous turncoats. Indeed their record has been brilliant thus far. As I said, it seems that every successful Christian rock group must take its show to the broader public. In fact, I chose them because of [their] sparkling record ...

Nevertheless, he discounted Pillar's new contract with a major label, which broadened its fan base and allowed the band to visit more secular gutters:

> Pillar's contract with Geffen means that they will have to tour with people who stand for very different things than they do. This can send mixed signals to the audience. [Singer Rob] Beckey explained, "I don't have the same beliefs as Godsmack, but I love their music." I know that Jesus ate with tax collectors and other sinners, but performing in godless venues could serve to weaken Pillar's witness ...[2]

Notice that? "*Could* serve to weaken" their witness. Now, I think this guy's heart is ultimately in the right place, but he's discounting the band when he makes statements like that. What Christian *isn't* presented with opportunities to weaken his or her witness? Every day I run across some situation that *could* weaken my witness. So do you. But that doesn't mean it happens.

I have known Rob and the guys in Pillar for more than four years now, and since the day I met them, I've been impressed both by their music

---

2. Keith Miller, "Pillar Crossing Over: What Must Christian Bands Be Careful of When Crossing Over to the Secular Market?" July 21, 2003, *www.evangelsociety.org/miller/pillar.html.*

and their love for Christ. I recently spent some time with them at a music festival and talked to Rob extensively about the band, and he told me that with their new label home, they've changed their approach while keeping their desire and purpose the same.

What is that desire? What is that purpose? The guys understand that their performance itself will only influence people thirty to sixty minutes a night on stage. To Rob, performing night after night seems more like his job than his ministry. Instead of the music, Rob's ministry is found through the relationships he establishes with people he comes in contact with daily.

It hasn't always been that way, though. When the band started, Rob would get onstage and preach, share, explain every song. But he was only doing that because that's what people were telling him Pillar needed to be doing, that this was what their ministry must look like. One evening, a youth pastor cornered Rob before the show and told him something a little strange. He said God had told him to tell Rob to tell the audience about Christ and to make sure he allowed students an opportunity to accept Christ during the performance that night.

Rob did the sensible thing and suggested that since this guy was so clear this Gospel presentation was from God, maybe he should be the one to make it. He realized then how many Christians often put their beliefs or opinions on someone else, or use another Christian's platform to get across their own opinions. From that night on, Pillar shifted its ministry focus from being on the stage to off the stage.

I asked Rob to define Pillar's gutter, and without any hesitation he said, "backstage." The reason Michael Francisco tells his audience that Chevelle shouldn't play at Ozzfest is the very same thing that excites Rob and the guys in Pillar. It is backstage at their shows where they have made contacts with Sevendust, Taproot, Slipknot, and Linkin Park. Like

Chevelle, Pillar has been able to shine Christ's light in one of the darkest spiritual places on earth: backstage at a rock concert.

They don't limit their gutter ministry to the bands they tour with. One night they played some martini bar in Texas, and after their set, when they were heading out the door, the security guard stopped them and said, "You guys are Christians, right? What do you think about praying?" Through that little open window, they began to talk with the guard about prayer and about Christ, and Kalel, the bass player, wound up praying with the guy that night.

My guess is that the guys at the Evangel Society would have a problem with Pillar playing a bar, but check out how God worked. They spoke to someone at a bar who wasn't even really listening to the band that night. This is a guy who has probably seen hundreds of bands as he watches the door every night—but there was something different about the Pillar guys that sparked his interest. Maybe he'd been wondering about prayer already. Maybe he'd been thinking about Jesus lately, or maybe that was the first time it'd ever crossed his mind. I don't know what made this security guard stop the guys on their way out, other than he saw something different about them. That's what the gutter is all about.

Rob told me about a conversation he had one night with Mac Powell, the lead singer of the popular Christian band Third Day. They had a long chat and finally came to this conclusion about their personal ministries: Their job is to create an environment where God, not they themselves, can move. In the long run, they simply have to be true to God and to His calling and allow Him to move in whatever way He deems necessary.

When it comes to the gutter backstage, and really the gutter at large, you must be willing to go where most people have not gone or say they cannot go. Sure, it's risky, but you have to take risks, especially if you're passionate about something. If you think about it too much, you might wind up scaring yourself out of it.

Now that his band has achieved some popularity, Rob has realized that no one in the media really talks about all the stuff that goes on behind the scenes, and while he is fine with that, he thinks people should take a look at what the band is actually doing before they start to level criticism against them.

Rob spends a lot of time in the gutter, but since he's a public figure, he has checks in place to make sure he keeps his nose clean, like the three different guys back home who help keep him accountable. He knows he can always talk with them about tough issues, keeping each other on their game. He also notes that the other guys in Pillar are great sources of encouragement to him, and he to them. They help each other out. This type of safety net is crucial for a lifestyle of going to the gutter.

One night about a year ago, my cell phone rang. I answered and found myself talking to Rob. He said he needed to talk to me because he'd let me down; I didn't know what he was talking about and asked him to explain. See, Rob struggled in the past with pornography, so he has a heart for those in the porn gutter. Pillar has a couple of songs about it on their albums, and Rob has shared his personal testimony on a video we did for XXXchurch. So with all that, Pillar has become a great voice for our ministry, talking about us at its shows and afterward.

But on this particular night, Rob was talking directly to me, telling me about a time a few months ago that he'd given in to temptation and fallen back into porn. He'd already talked to his wife and his accountability partners about it, but he said he still felt horrible, like he'd let XXXchurch down and that he couldn't play another show without talking to me about it. We talked for a while and wound up ending the conversation just a few minutes before Pillar took the stage that night. Rob felt unburdened and ready to go back into the gutter.

As the night went on, I thought more and more about that phone call. The more I thought about it, the more respect I gained for Rob and the rest of the guys in the band—these guys represent the type of people we want in the gutter: honest, open, real, and transparent. I don't know too many lead singers who are weighed down minutes before a show thinking about sins they've committed, or really any of them who would openly confess to something like this.

The last time Pillar came through this part of town, I hopped on its tour bus after the show and found a youth pastor from Wisconsin on board. But his youth group wasn't in tow—they were still at home while this man was serving as a road pastor for the band. Yep. Pillar has its very own pastor on the road. It's not something you hear about very often, because most people—including Internet scribes—don't see what goes on in the tour bus, but I'm glad Pillar has the smarts to head into the gutter with the right perspective.

And when they get in the gutter, they know how to speak the language. Rob spent years in the gutter—trapped there. A drug addict, he threw away opportunity after opportunity, including a college scholarship, so he could lounge around in the gutter. He finally cleaned up and now has a viable ministry backstage at secular concerts, where drugs run wild. Since he knows what it's like and knows the consequences of that lifestyle, he can fluently speak the language of that gutter.

(In case you're worried for him, Rob says he can go into that gutter and not be tempted to revert back to his old ways because he specifically asked God for the ability to do just that—and God answered his request.)

I asked Rob how important the gutter was, and this was his take: "There are so many people who just don't get it. A big reason why people are not going to the gutter is because so many of them don't know what they believe or why. They're just a 'Christian.' But getting out among the people and experiencing things is the best way to find out where God wants you to be."

He takes it a step further and likens the modern Church to an aquarium. It's decorated nicely, kept clean, and contains only fish that get along with each other, ultimately becoming so pleasant that no one wants to leave. But lest we forget—there is an ocean called "the real world," a place where fish don't always get along, where bad things can and do happen.

We've heard the rallying cry over and over again, to be *in* the world, but not *of* the world. But how can you even be in the world if you don't go to the world? When Jesus told us to go into the world, He didn't mean we needed to sit around talking about it, or read books about it, or bring it up at the next board meeting—He meant for us to go, to smash the walls of our pretty little aquariums and start swimming in the ocean.

"I think Jesus is proud of aggressive Christians," Rob said. "The Pauls, the Peters, the Barnabases ... people who are aggressively pursuing the kingdom of God. I think Jesus stands up when He sees that type of aggressiveness. You know, the only time the Bible mentions Jesus standing at the right hand of God is when Stephen was being stoned (Acts 7:55). Stephen had shown aggressiveness, and I think we show that when we head to the gutter. And I think Jesus stands up for us then."

There's another band that typifies going to the backstage gutter—a little outfit known as P.O.D. These guys are the real deal, and they still get frustrated by over-righteous Christians. I even found a website detailing how P.O.D. is just plain evil that came with this disclaimer: "There are parts of the section 'P.O.D. AND THE WORKS OF DARKNESS' that are not recommended for some Christians. We have cleaned it up for Christian viewing as much as possible, but because of the subject matter, there are parts that some may find offensive."

How sad that things have to be "cleaned up for Christian viewing." This is the antithesis of the gutter mentality.

Last holiday season I attended the biggest show of the year: KROQ's (*the* rock station in Los Angeles) Annual Acoustic Christmas show. I go to this concert just about every year (I've attended five of the last seven), mainly because it's the most consistently amazing show produced anywhere. But this year I was especially stoked because three of the bands on the bill were bands made up of Christians. The lineup included:

12/13/2003
Linkin Park
The Offspring
P.O.D.
AFI
Puddle Of Mudd
Pennywise
Chevelle
The Distillers
Thrice

This list is what the gutter looks like. A sold-out show, the most listened-to rock station in L.A. and a whole bunch of the year's biggest bands. It's big, it's popular; and it's full of people on both sides of the curtain who need Jesus.

I went with my friend Eric, and our tickets included a "backstage" pass, so we tooled down Universal in the Porn Mobile and arrived in time to catch Thrice. After they played their set, we decided it was still early (5 p.m.) and we had a long night ahead of us, *so*, we thought, *why not head backstage?*

But backstage wasn't really *backstage*. It was just a cool little meet-and-greet area with a cash bar, some free cookies, and a ton of people who wanted to be part of the cool backstage crowd. We took in the scene, munching some cookies and playing a little Xbox. (Yes, I shelled out money to go "backstage" and play video games—for some reason it was cooler than just doing it at my house.) As we watched people interact with each other, we began to notice how shallow and fake the whole scene was.

Now that we knew what was happening in our limited backstage area, we left to check out another band. Throughout the night, we kept going backstage, just because we could. I don't know what we were expecting to see, but we enjoyed the power of immediate backstage access, and we took full advantage of it. Even though there was nothing for us back there (the cookies were gone after the second band), we still kept going, just because we could.

After P.O.D. played (an awesome show), we went backstage for the final time to tell them "hi." Hanging in the semi-cool backstage area, I realized I had to use the restroom, so I started to look around for one. And wouldn't you know it, I found a sign instead—a sign that said, "LINKIN PARK BACKSTAGE/DRESSING ROOMS" with an arrow pointing to the right.

The secret had been revealed, and since we realized how worthless our backstage was, we decided to go for it. We made a run for the door and followed Linkin Park's signs all the way back to their dressing room—*the* backstage. The gutter. It made the fake backstage gutter look like a kindergarten class. There were nine individual dressing rooms for each band, complete with a room for hanging out and an outdoor dining/grill area. Once a band performed, they started to party, and it was pretty crazy. Sex, drugs, and rock 'n' roll: all three and more, free for the taking.

When P.O.D. emerged from their dressing room, my respect, admiration, and love for the band grew even more. I was getting a glimpse of something hardly anyone sees, and while I'd resorted to sneaking in to do it, P.O.D. had earned the right to be there, musically and spiritually. It was a humbling thing to hear P.O.D.'s voice in that deep, deep gutter. Sure, they'd put on a rad show (and most of the Christians in the audience were probably hoping for some more "Jesus" plugs), but their gutter isn't about the show—it's about having an impact here, in the true backstage gutter, among people who are influencing millions through music.

Eric and I just hung out for a short while, totally impressed by the respect and love all the pre-Christian bands had for the P.O.D. guys. I could tell that though they didn't hold the same beliefs as the rest of the bands there, the P.O.D. guys still had built solid relationships. They weren't scared to go into that gutter; instead, they went in full force in an effort to have a sizable impact, if only by abstaining from the behavior going on back there.

When Christian bands attempt to cross over or become popular, a lot of religious people get scared and start to throw stones instead of supporting these brothers and sisters in Christ. Then they watch the bands with a radar to make sure they are going to live up to the name of Christ. That night, I realized that music ministry isn't about the number of times you say "Jesus" in a song or in your liner notes or from the stage—it's about an everyday witness and a willingness to step into that gutter. It's about earning the right to be heard.

And it works the same with any gutter. You can't go into the gutter until you've figured out what you believe and why—so that you know you won't be swayed by the gutter. Not everyone is called to go to a porn show like me, and not everyone is called to be a big successful band like P.O.D.—but everyone is called to a gutter. And when you go, you will be challenged by what you find. You stand the chance of being ridiculed or mocked. But if you stay true to Jesus and true to the gifts He's given to you, you'll earn the right to speak to that gutter. And you will have an impact.

I started this chapter with a quote from a member of Stryper, so it only makes sense that I end it talking about the man who helped Stryper reach its gutter. His name is Michael Guido, and he became Stryper's road pastor before Stryper was even a household name. Tim Gaines brought him to the garage/rehearsal studio where the band practiced, and when they began to open up their rehearsals for the neighborhood kids, Guido would share in between songs and speak to the assembled people about Christ.

Guido had a successful tile business, but his heart was for the gutter. He began to travel with the band, footing his own bill so he could serve God in whatever capacity he could. Of course, Stryper folded up their tents a long time ago, but Guido didn't. Since his time with Stryper, Guido has been road pastor to many other bands and now ministers to P.O.D. and Blindside, among others—always out of a desire to get into the backstage gutter.

Can we all agree that Guido knows a thing or two about the gutter? Here's a guy who spent the first part of his life in the gutter, living in the world and the lust of the flesh, not knowing where he was going to end up. Then God stepped in, bringing him out of the gutter just so he could go back into it, this time on God's side. So now he's spent the rest of his life, and a good deal of his own money, going back, and you know what he says about it? He says it doesn't matter how God delivers us—just that He does it. Listen, God can deliver anyone from anywhere, but He can't deliver anyone from the gutter if we as a Church don't take Him there.

Guido says that nothing can sway his confidence in God, so he has no problem going into the gutter to see what God will do there. He was recently on a tour with Blindside, and literally forty-five minutes into the tour, the band crashed its bus. But instead of being swayed, his confidence was only confirmed by the incident, and that confidence had already rubbed off on the band—Simon, the guitarist, said, "We must be doing something right." When you go to the gutter, you must go on the foundation of Christ. If you build differently—on His foundation—then you can stand anywhere. Build on sand and circumstances, like the rest of those in the gutter, and you'll eventually fall down.

Guido has been working with bands in the backstage gutter for twenty years—not because he loves music (although he does), but because he loves the gutter, and he loves encouraging people to get into the gutter. I asked him how he decides which bands to work with, and he said the first thing he does is ask his teenage kids who they're listening to, because he wants to reach the people who are having an impact on his kids. Then he starts to pray for those bands, asking God whether he should have a part in their lives. God will either confirm it or hold off on answering until the time is right to reveal His will. But whatever the answer, Guido always is available. He knows he's truly called to the gutter.

At this point in our conversation, Guido read me Isaiah 49. The whole thing. It's a bit long to reprint here, but you should check it out before you read any further. This is what Guido said God has been teaching him lately, and that it's already had an effect on the band he's working with right now. They had all their passports and cash stolen at the end of the tour—it was a disaster—but he said they came back from the gutter with Isaiah 49 imprinted on their foreheads. That's why he's still in the game.

According to Guido, the modern Church stays out of the gutter the same way the Pharisees stayed away from the unrighteous. Sometimes we just think we're better than them, or we're afraid we might revert back to our old gutter-based lifestyle. But where is our compassion for the lost? Peter and Paul, at the end of their lives, weren't bragging about their place in the Church—they were still broken for the lost. Jesus continually showed compassion for those in the gutter.

And that's what Guido encourages in the artists he works with. He knows that lyrics are just the outer layer of real ministry, and he's seen bands talk for hours with people in the gutter and offstage. He says, "We want to put God in a box, but He doesn't fit in a box. Most of the bands I work with don't fit in a box—that's why they're in the gutter."

We are all called to do something, and we can't put price tags on those callings—we must keep to the calling, like Paul admonishes. It can't just be words on our part—we must be living out our calling, we must put the words into action. We must be compelled by the love of Christ to complete our calling and get into the gutter. Allow it to push us in and drive us back.

Guido tempers this fervency with a reminder that not everyone is called to the same gutter. "There was John the Baptist and John the beloved disciple. Both have the same name, but very different callings to particular gutters. One is no better than the other—they're just two different people each responding to their callings and being obedient and thankful to what God had entrusted them to do."

It's very easy to sit on the sidelines and criticize those who are going into the gutter so publicly, like musicians. But if we aren't willing to go into the gutter, we must at least support our brothers and sisters in their efforts to go, instead of wasting our time picking apart their every action.

Guido quotes 1 Corinthians 4:5: "Therefore judge nothing before the appointed time; wait till the Lord comes. He will bring to light what is hidden in darkness and will expose the motives of men's hearts. At that time each will receive his praise from God."

The bottom line: We will only be judged on our motives and our purpose. My prayer is that the Church wakes up and gets the right motive—to reach into the gutter for the sole purpose of lifting up Christ. Then the gutter-dwellers will be drawn to Him, and our mission will be one step closer to completion.

# 11
# THE GUTTER AT MIDNIGHT

## CHAPTER ELEVEN

The midnight hour holds a certain reputation. Growing up as a kid, I knew that if I could just stay awake until midnight, I would have arrived. It was the time of *Saturday Night Live*, *Headbangers Ball*, and the scary movies, but I rarely managed to stay awake that long.

These days, I rarely go to sleep before midnight. It makes for interesting outings. Oftentimes while traveling, I'll go out and find myself sitting in diners, coffee shops, or other late-night dives like Waffle House, Denny's, blah blah blah. They're all the same—great places to eat crummy food and kill a little time while waiting for sleep to overtake me.

But there are others who find better ways to spend this time, late as the hour might be, with valuable, impacting outreach. Jason, a longtime friend of XXXchurch, who lives in northern California, leads a ministry program for college-aged students called Master's Commission, and he recently told me a story that blew my mind. I'd heard some incredible outreach stories before, but as we met for coffee at one of our speaking engagements, Jason told me a story about the midnight gutter that changed me in a way none other had.

It's the story of Reverend Bob Johnson and the City Ministries of San Francisco, often referred to as that city's Dream Center. It's the story of Night Strikes, a Friday night outreach to the Tenderloin area of San Francisco. It's the story, plain and simple, of the gutter.

Every Friday night, rain or shine, hot or cold, Reverend Johnson and his team gather at United Nations Square to prepare for that evening's ministry. They sing a few songs, hear a few words of encouragement, and then lead people like Jason into the midnight gutter. Jason had always loved a ministry challenge, but this night was different. It was the weekend before Halloween, Satan's play-day weekend, so it felt as though perversion pounded the streets a little more strongly.

As they headed out, the crisp San Francisco air brought a pointed chill to Jason's face. Confusion overwhelmed him as his team formed and began to head out. As he walked with his group toward Polk Street, questions of ministry purpose flooded his mind.

Polk is notorious for being loaded with street workers, transvestites, transsexuals, and runaway teens. Jason didn't know it at the moment, but as they headed north from Polk onto Post, his life began to change. They met the first of many in the midnight gutter there, perched on the corner, leaning against the wall. They approached, and the prostitute stood up as if to let them know what was for sale.

"Coco" had officially entered his life.

Jason's heart pounded. He asked himself, "What am I doing here?" It was 11:30 p.m. and along with six others, the team was running a recovery operation for the kingdom of God to San Francisco's Red Light District. More specifically, the gutter. Jason felt like he didn't belong there, that maybe the challenge was too great. From a distance, he looked into the prostitute's eyes and saw a tattered gate made of splintered wood with rusted hinges. A broken-down soul. Coco represented one of hundreds of street workers in San Francisco—men and women, boys and girls—who use the sex industry to get by in life.

All this happened in the blink of an eye, and as Jason led his team a little closer to Coco, he noticed a man coming from the opposite direction. A man who looked very much out of place, dressed nicely and looking eager. Of course, Jason and his team looked out of place, too.

They approached Coco simultaneously, Jason's team and the nicely dressed man, each with a different agenda. The man hoped for an illicit rendezvous; Jason hoped to communicate the love of God in a real and authentic way. It became apparent there was going to be a showdown.

The man got to Coco first, and Jason immediately thought of abandoning the mission. He couldn't decide whether to back away or interrupt Coco's "business." Then he sensed the man's nervousness, and a boldness arose in him—he started forward to speak to Coco, though the man had already begun his subtle offer. There was no way Jason would let this moment slip past him.

Through his boldness, fear crept in. Not fear of what to say or how to say it, but fear of actually speaking to a real-live prostitute on the street. Hookers had come to his different outreaches before, but this was different. He was uninvited and on Coco's turf. He was in the gutter at midnight. Nevertheless, he cleared his throat and spoke to Coco in a soft voice, "Ma'am, what I would like to offer you will have a greater eternal value than what he's offering." With that one sentence, Jason had Coco's attention, and the nameless man began to slink away down a side street.

Jason continued, offering a pink rose. "May I give you this rose?" Shocked and confused, Coco did not answer. "I would like to give you this rose to illustrate to you that this is the way God created you. You are special to Him, and He loves you." Still silent, Coco agreed to take the rose, but when Jason asked if he could pray for protection, the prostitute simply replied, "No."

They exchanged smiles. Coco said, "Thank you," and walked away. Jason felt he had failed. Until he realized something about the rose.

Conducting business for the rest of the night, things would have to be different. Coco would probably toss the rose on a broken nightstand in a motel room that rents by the hour. The rose was cheap; its monetary value was probably less than eighty cents. But its significance was priceless. Most likely, Coco would pick it up upon leaving the dirty room, perhaps keeping it all night long. As Coco did "business," the value of this prostitute's existence screamed through that silent, beautiful rose. This stranded gutter-dweller did, in fact, matter to God.

Jason and the Sacramento team walked away from Coco knowing at least one trick had been derailed. The simplicity of a rose spoke volumes about God's love for this lonely street worker. A rose offered by a man was symbolic of a gift given from the Son of Man.

On the way back to City Ministries, Jason was quiet. Even in the early morning hours after midnight, Polk bustled with activity. Jason began to think about his own family, back home, hours away. He'd get home late that night, wake up in the morning to the sounds of his children playing. They'd spend the day playing, take a trip to Wal-Mart, and stop for a lunch appointment at McDonald's.

But his peaceful thinking was interrupted when he thought about Coco. Coco was somebody's child, but somewhere along the line, the prostitute had been disregarded and disgraced to the point of finding *his* only dwelling place on Polk Street.

Coco was someone's *son.*

Did his parents know where he was? Or even worse, did they care? Jason doubted Coco's parents had planned his life to unfold this way, but the plans of parents didn't matter now. Coco was grown up, and he was on the streets.

How did he get here? Maybe it was his fault, maybe not. People in the midnight gutter have often been dumped there through abuse, rape, or incest. According to The Council for Prostitution Alternatives' Annual Report for 1994, 85 percent of prostitutes reported a history of sexual abuse in childhood; 70 percent reported incest. Is that an excuse for their behavior? No, but maybe it's part of the reason. Regardless of how Coco got there, the fact remains: It's midnight, and he needs Jesus.

Sometimes it's hard to summon sympathy for a prostitute. I know I've had a hard time in the past. Add to it the fact that many are homosexuals, transvestites, or transsexuals, and finding compassion for them can be downright difficult. You can understand why Jason felt trepidation about approaching Coco. But that person is somebody's baby; that person is God's baby.

I've felt the hardness of the church pews when I've asked others to go out to the gutter to minister with me, not far away to San Francisco, but right in our home city. Most times I hear, "No thanks," or, "I'm busy at that time," or the most common one, "I'm not called to them." I'm sure that's accurate in a lot of cases, but on occasion, what they're really saying is, "They're not my responsibility." Aren't they?

# CHAPTER ELEVEN

Jesus said that what I do to the least of our society, I've done to Him. Quite frankly, I can't think of many people groups who I would least like to reach out to: cross-dressing prostitutes, homosexuals, or transsexuals. The Cocos. Yet despite the people group, the subculture, or the hedonistic display of miserable sin, Coco is still someone Jesus loves.

The sin. The perversion. The gutter. It's grotesque. Sometimes, it's overwhelming to the point where we freeze up. Yet we must go. We must be willing to speak to the Cocos of this world with the love of a saving Christ. If we don't go to them, how else will we be able to minister to the least of them? How else will we be able to minister like Jesus did?

Some would say, "Well, brother, I am not called to that place." When Jesus spoke of ministering to people, He wasn't speaking of an exclusive geographic location—He meant the people who are out there in society. People on the highways and byways of culture, people I've driven past without the slightest concern for their eternity. People in the midnight gutter.

Not every midnight gutter appears in the Red Light District; many times you can find gutter-dwellers in the least likely venues, places that can stretch your theology. Your backyard, your family, your workplace, your whatever. It's no less a gutter than the Red Light District. Imagine going to the midnight gutter and rescuing people out of the restaurant chain called Hooters.

Based mainly in the Southeast United States, Hooters' has an owl as its mascot. Get it? "Hoot"-ers. But only the most naïve of us don't get the double meaning of the restaurant's name upon learning that the waitresses wear tight-fitting T-shirts and short shorts. Their menu is simple, and they stay open until midnight. So out of desperation to meet the lost where they were, Nelson Foster (no relation to Mike) of Single Focus Atlanta created the Hooters Outreach.

After spending years on church staffs, Nelson and his son started looking for public places to talk about life and life's issues with other men. They had a desire to meet late at night, and with limited options for a venue, Hooters gave them a quiet, outside porch. It was simply a relaxed place that met the need. That was five years ago, and now the Hooters Outreach is a success, reaching unchurched men who would never darken the door of the local church.

It may not be how you would do it. It may not be where you would do it. But *they are doing it*. The packaging is troubling for many, but for the Fosters, it just made sense. They go into a gutter where God can meet men.

The Hooters Outreach was not, and still is not, designed to be a Bible study. Every Thursday night at 10:00 p.m., Hooters became the place to talk about life and all that goes on in it. Sure, Bible topics came up during the talk times, but it has remained discussion-driven and based on life issues. From these issues, the facilitator brings truth from a biblical perspective. Life has emerged from the gutter.

Regular restaurant patrons were the first to ask questions. Would there be a worship time with singing or a deep prayer time? Actually, no. Sure, they have other ministry environments that offer Bible studies, worship, and prayer times, but not at Hooters. If someone needed prayer, the team prayed right there. No one shied away from that spiritual aspect, but they remained committed to defining the outreach as anything but a church service.

Inevitably, the seeds planted in this needy environment will become the starting point for something else. Just like Mike and I with XXXchurch, Nelson and his team were willing to go to the gutter and mix the seedy with the sacred. Although it is advertised as a discussion group, the structure is free flowing, and the vision has always been simply to reach people where they are. With that vision, they have had challenges, including one very severe incident that happened one evening on the way to the Hooters outreach. Nelson was killed by a drunk driver.

Deprived suddenly of its leader, the group faced a crossroads. Fortunately, sub-leadership among the regular attendees had already been established, and now it was time for one of them to step up. That man was Rick Lamborn. Rick was a faithful volunteer who was willing to be part of an outreach nearly everyone in the church despised. Rick built on the foundation Nelson had established and found great inroads with the restaurant.

Initially, the Hooters staff was leery. Imagine that. Hooters was concerned about what the Christians would do during their Life Perspective discussion time, worried they would be inviting in a bunch of Pastor Bibles who would judge the patrons instead of having a passion for the soul inside. But Nelson, Rick, and the rest of the Hooters Outreach did nothing but love people. They led the group with consistency, dedication, and consideration, choosing to talk *to* people instead of *at* them. The group then spread to a Mexican restaurant and a sports club in their efforts to broaden their impact.

"Why not McDonald's?," skeptics ask. Rick is very quick to point out that Mickey D's would be a great place to have a discussion group ... if they had targeted soccer moms with kids. Rick and his team know they could have a great impact at lunchtime at McDonald's, but that's simply not the gutter they're called to reach.

In the summer of 2004, a local news channel found out about the outreach, and news spread quickly. As you may have guessed, gutter-denying Christians began to protest, coming out in full force with picket signs. (Unfortunately for them, they came on the wrong night. Go figure. Christians picketing other Christians at Hooters on the wrong night.)

It's amazing to see Rick's commitment through all this chaos. When I talked to him, he made sure I knew he isn't an ordained pastor. Instead, he's just someone with a heart for reaching people in the gutter ... that gutter being bars, sports clubs, and any other areas to reach people who are pre-Christians.

The goal for the outreach has always been to evangelize—to get pre-Christians into a local church while simultaneously getting the local church into the community. The idea remains that people can be reached, restored, raised, and then released back into the outreach flow. Before this successful outreach, who would have ever believed Hooters could be a usable venue for mentoring and discipleship? Yet it has been, and continues to be, as Rick and the rest of his team reach into the Hooters gutter and encourage people to pursue a relationship with God.

Christ did it. No, there was no Jerusalem version of Hooters, but Jesus did connect with society's hurting, neglected population. He reached out to the least of them, not the popular and the powerful. He reached the midnight gutter, and sure enough, the religious raised red flags.

Rick has seen the same red flags, but instead of hyper-righteous Pharisees condemning him to his face, he's mostly getting criticism from the online community (the same as XXXchurch does). Below are just a few of the indictments Rick faced when the story of his gutter outreach, titled "On a Wing and a Prayer," appeared online:

> I was shocked when I read, "On a Wing and a Prayer." To think that someone is holding a Bible study at Hooters of all places. Do you even know what the name "Hooters" implies?

> As a minister I hold to the more traditional ways of reaching the lost, such as visitation programs, radio broadcasts, supporting missionary ministries, etc. Mixing a little of the Gospel with worldly issues in a

sexually charged atmosphere is not what we as Christians are called to do. You need to ask yourself, "Would I hold a church service here?" If you can honestly answer yes, then you need to also ask yourself, "Am I truly saved?"

Please understand that I am not brow-beating you. I am just concerned with the light that this type of thing sheds on God's Church. I will be praying for you and hope that you will consider my letter seriously.

\* \* \* \* \*

Hello. I've just read ["On a Wing and a Prayer"]. I cannot believe you would choose to take youth who in postmodern society find it increasingly difficult to keep a pure thought-life and avoid sexual immorality, and subject them to so-called Bible studies at Hooters, of all places. As a normal male in his 30s, I can tell you right now if I were at one of those meetings, it wouldn't be the Bible I was studying! I can also guarantee you a number of the young men at your meetings are struggling with lust, while a number of the young women are comparing themselves to the buxom waitresses. What a stupid thing to do, to place them in that kind of lust-feeding environment.

It's always legitimate to pursue an "Incarnation" model of outreach in which we "meet unbelievers where they're at"—but not while simultaneously subjecting ourselves to unnecessary temptation. There are all sorts of outreach opportunities that could be pursued without going to Hooters. Good grief, you people are out of your minds. And I'm sure some are out of their minds with *lust*, but just haven't admitted it.

\* \* \* \* \*

Hooters? You all need to understand the mindset of a man. I can attest to the struggle of keeping a pure heart. It involves daily discipline, which comes from constant prayer. Being a twenty-five-year-old who has had problems with lust in my past, I will tell you that no man, not even a Christian, can resist the temptation of a half-naked woman. You set these young men up for failure, and you will be held responsible when the time comes. I pray for you.

Rick has heard it all from the judge and jury of the religious ones. The issue within the Church is that many of us want to be armchair quarterbacks, relying on what we believe is the best (and only) way to reach people. Many struggle with the incorrect perception that if an outreach method doesn't fit into our box of beliefs, then it is either sinful or corrupt.

Is it not feasible to believe that God's Word is true? The Bible says that God has chosen the weak and foolish things of this world to confound the wise and mighty (1 Cor. 1:27). You may think the Hooters Outreach is a foolish and weak approach. It may offend you. It may offend your church. I understand. But at midnight, the stakes are high. At midnight, the parameters of what appears to be right in your sight are a non-issue. At midnight, a critical, judgmental opinion is worthless—all that counts is that the midnight gutter matters to God.

I just quoted 1 Corinthians 1:27, but take a look at the full passage, verses 26-31:

> Take a good look, friends, at who you were when you got called into this life. I don't see many of "the brightest and the best" among you, not many influential, not many from high-society families. Isn't it obvious that God deliberately chose men and women that the culture overlooks and exploits and abuses, chose these "nobodies" to expose the hollow pretensions of the "somebodies"? That makes it quite clear

that none of you can get by with blowing your own horn before God. Everything that we have—right thinking and right living, a clean slate and a fresh start—comes from God by way of Jesus Christ. That's why we have the saying, "If you're going to blow a horn, blow a trumpet for God." (MES)

I encourage you to pause for a moment to pray. Ask God to soften any critical mindset you may have, a mindset that sets up judgments against something that might stretch your outreach theology. You don't have to serve at the Hooters Outreach; just don't judge it. God may or may not use it—that's up to Him. He can take an unconventional method and use it to communicate an unchanging Gospel, but He has difficulty using a critical heart.

We have been given a mandate for the midnight hour. Whether it's Coco in the Tenderloin of San Francisco or Bible talks at skintight burger joints, the midnight gutters are sometimes just plain awkward. But time always passes, and midnight will always give way to morning.

That's when joy comes (Ps. 30:5). The joy of real and authentic love emerging through the risen Son. The question for Christians is not whether God can have an impact in the gutter. It's whether you and I will go.

Time passes.

The midnight hour is at hand for those in the gutter.

Check your watch and discover for your own soul ... what time is it?

# 12

## THE GUTTER-FORGED GREATNESS ... WILL YOU GO?

### CHAPTER TWELVE

Dallas. October 2004. I was at the National Youth Workers Convention, sponsored by Youth Specialties, in town to talk about porn and to show a sneak preview of *Missionary Positions*. Coincidentally, this was all taking place the same weekend as the annual "Red River Rivalry" game between the University of Oklahoma and the University of Texas, played every year in Dallas at the Cotton Bowl. It's a huge deal, and fans come from far and wide to support their teams.

Starting to get the idea? Nearly 3,200 youth workers. Roughly 70,000 football fans. And as far as I could tell, we were all staying in the same hotel, the Adam's Mark. Most of us youth convention attendees were in the north tower, most of the football fans were in the south. My family and I were coming back to the hotel from dinner, and as we got on our elevator to head up to our room, I noticed the line to get on the elevator to the south tower was full of Oklahoma-T-shirt-wearing college students ready for a full night of partying, partying, and more partying. Gutter living in a swank hotel.

I slept fine that night, and the next morning as I walked to breakfast, I noticed a long line at the registration desk, but not full of students—it was full of conference attendees who'd been stuck with the college students in the south tower. They were desperately begging to move their room so they could get some sleep the next night. But no luck—the hotel was booked to 100-percent capacity, so they'd just have to live with it until the fans started leaving Sunday morning.

Now it's 10:30 a.m., and I'm in General Session #3, taking place in the hotel's second-floor ballroom. I'd wandered in to see what was up and found the joint jumping as 3,200 youth workers participated in corporate worship. The worship leader instructed them to hold hands and "sing and dance like the saved." (Lucky for me, I was on the sideline and therefore didn't have to hold hands.)

So here it was: 3,200 youth workers singing so loudly and dancing so hard that the floor began to shake. They were making such a ruckus I began to wonder if the room could handle this kind of intensity. Finally, they settled down, a speaker shared, a comedian tried to be funny, another band played even louder, and two hours later the crowd was dismissed for lunch.

But while they were dancing and singing and moving the floor, I noticed something wrong with the picture I was seeing. General Session #3 was great and all, but why are there 3,200 people at this conference learning to be better youth workers while simultaneously requesting to be farther away from the YOUTH surrounding them?

For some of these workers, conferences like this are a vacation, a time to get away from their kids back home and just relax, and I have no problem with that. But you'd think that in a room of 3,200 people who specialize in reaching young students, there would have been *some* rumblings among them as they devised ways to reach the gutter youth joining us this weekend.

What if General Session #3 had been held in the stadium parking lot? Seventy-thousand-plus fans, many of them students, all tailgating before the game. We could interact with these people and get a peek into their world. Step into their gutter, whatever it may be.

What if, instead of complaining about all the noise the night before and requesting new rooms, the people in the south tower realized the opportunity in front of them? Sure, college students aren't usually part of the job description of most youth pastors, but many of these kids were once in youth group. Maybe they didn't get reached then, but could get reached now.

What if we all got it through our heads that seminars, workshops, and gatherings are great, but *people* are even better? Christian comedy and outrageous ice-breaking games are fine things to take back to your youth group, but I can think of something even better: Real-life illustrations of how God didn't just bring a great speaker or workshop to the convention, but how He put you in contact with some young people from the gutter.

Three thousand, two hundred of us could have had a major impact on the gutter, but we chose to hang around each other instead. What a blown opportunity.

There are opportunities all around us if we'll just take the time to look for them. Sometimes the opportunities are sitting right in front of us, and we almost have to turn the other way not to see them. My life was greatly impacted by a woman who simply did what was in front of her to do. Her name was Marie.

Marie was in her late 70s and living in a retirement home when I met her. Born and raised in the Bronx, New York, she had only come out to California at the insistence of her son. She and her husband were too old to care for one another anymore, so out they'd come to Fullerton to live with their youngest. Just a week into their arrival, Marie had a stroke while walking up the stairs, blacking out and tumbling all the way down to land with a thump on the first floor.

She spent some time in the hospital, and when she'd finally healed, she discovered that her son wasn't as ready for the responsibility as he'd thought and had secured living quarters for her in a nursing home. She was wheelchair-bound but determined to walk again, and she didn't understand his reasoning; nevertheless, she had to accept it, and that's how she found herself at Acacia Villa Retirement Home.

It was a nice place, but Marie hated it immediately. She thought it was full of a bunch of "loonies" and wanted nothing to do with life among the residents. Unsure of what to do with the remainder of her life and time, and figuring she had nothing to lose, she began to smoke like a champ. Now, Marie loved to smoke, but this time smoking gave her something to do, and it was a reminder of her life before she moved to California.

But there was a catch. Marie wasn't allowed to smoke inside the building, so in a fit of rage, she informed the nurses that she would eat and sleep inside, but other than that, she was going to live outside on the sidewalk. Everyone thought she was joking, but Marie meant every word, and the staff soon found out how serious she was. For the next six months, Marie's daily routine looked like this: out of bed around 6:30 a.m., then breakfast, then off to the sidewalk for the rest of the day. Rain or shine, it didn't matter to her; sometimes she didn't even go in for lunch.

The sidewalk was located at a busy intersection, and soon Marie tired of passively watching the cars go by. So she started waving to them. Now, when the retirement home staff saw her waving to every car that went by, they naturally assumed she'd lost her mind. But the reality, as Marie puts it, was that she would go nuts if she stayed inside all day. "I'm like a stinking piece of cheese," she once told me. "No one comes to see me or cares if I am alive, so if I can brighten up someone else's day by waving, then I guess that's why I'm here."

"I wouldn't wish my life upon anyone," Marie always said, and looking at her life, I could see why. She'd spent most of it in a loveless marriage to a gambling addict. Her mother had passed away when she was three. She had no relationship to speak of with her five children. Her life had been one long, hard, lonely road, and while she never wanted others to experience her life, she now had a desire to use it so others could gain. And so she used what was literally in front of her—her hand and oncoming traffic.

It wasn't long before Marie was a big hit. Motorists would honk as they drove to school, work, or wherever they were going. She would greet thousands of cars a week with a wave, and the majority of them would return the gesture with a honk. As Marie waved to more and more people, her notoriety grew until she was unofficially christened the new "Fullerton Town Greeter!"

One day I was driving down Chapman Avenue, and I will never forget seeing Marie on the side of the road waving at me. I knew right away this was my opportunity. I had seen this lady there before; how could I have missed her sitting right there on the side of the road? But this particular day, it was like it was the first day. I just knew I needed to stop and talk to her. That move changed my life. I never knew stopping that one day would turn into a three-year relationship with a lady in her late 70s, who would eventually become closer than family. Written here are some excerpts from a letter I wrote Marie.

> I was on my way to class, and I couldn't help noticing you sitting over there. I honked my horn and smiled as I drove by. Several days later you were still right there smiling and waving not just to me but also to everyone on Chapman Boulevard. So I decided I wanted to meet this nice lady who waved to me from the sidewalk. I got out of my car and nervously walked up behind you; you didn't see me coming until I shouted, "Hello there." You tried to sit up in your wheelchair and told me your name was Marie, and I said I just wanted to meet this lady who is always out here waving. That is when you told me your story. And you told me you couldn't remember the last time someone came to see you, not even your son.

That day, right then and there on Chapman Boulevard, I decided I would visit Marie each week. I promised her I would come back, and it was the beginning of a great friendship.

> I came back all right. How could I not? You were always so happy to see me. You tell it like it is. If you don't like someone, you'll be sure they know it. Like the time when I bleached my hair, or that one day I had to separate you and your roommate. I know she had it coming.

> The last two Thanksgivings were the best ever. We sat in that little room eating Boston Market, laughing and telling jokes. Well, you were telling most of the jokes, and most of them I couldn't repeat. Or that one day when we were sitting outside and you were yelling at the crossing guard. I don't remember his name, but you kept yelling, "Dopey, hey, Dopey." He tried to ignore you, but he couldn't help but smile as you kept yelling for the next ten minutes.

I will never forget my twenty-first birthday. I scored some extra cash and knew I would be getting some more since Christmas was in three days. I'd bought all my gifts and had already given you a box of sugar-free chocolates and a framed picture of us. I went by to see you on my birthday, and I remember you weren't outside because it was raining. You didn't look too happy in that room of yours. When I was in that room, I thought about Jesus' words, "Love your neighbor as yourself." I saw that the box of chocolate that cost me about $5 was almost gone, and I had $100 in my wallet. I told you I would be right back, and when I came back with that twenty-inch TV in my arms, you almost wet your pants. Well, I don't know about that. I just remember you starting to cry, but then you told every single person in that convalescent home about your new TV with remote control. Finally you could watch *Jeopardy!* in bed. "You don't know how much this means to me," that's what you said.

You never asked me for anything. That's why I was always so happy to give you whatever I could. Menthol cigarettes, chocolate candies, sugar-free gum and mints, and anything else you could manage to eat with those gums. That was the least I could do for you. I can't even begin to think of all the things I got in return. Flowers, stuffed animals, T-shirts, dolls, plants, pictures, clocks, blankets, and anything else the public gave you. You kept it all in a hidden place until I came by. Oh! And the bananas. I never told you that I don't even like bananas, but you were always so happy to give them to me. I remember you would ask for an extra one every night at dinner, not because you were hungry but so you could hide it for me. And as soon as I showed up, out they'd come, from the drawers, your wheelchair, the bathroom, and anywhere else you could hide them. "Get a bag," you'd say, "you know where they are." Out I would walk with four, five, six bananas in my bag. Sometimes I didn't even take them out of my jeep. I would just leave them in the car, and a couple days later I would start to smell something pretty ripe. I would smile because I knew those were your bananas you got especially for me.

I remember how much you loved my girlfriend, Jeanette, and how we both thought the world of you. After I proposed to Jeanette, I remember coming by your place and telling you the exciting news before anyone else. You were so happy for the both of us. We got in a little discussion, because you said you were not going to be able to come to the wedding because of your stupid wheelchair. I remember saying that I would come by the home early in the morning on my wedding day, and we would walk together the mile and a half down the road to go to the church. "Marie, you're coming, and you're sitting in the first row." You put up a fight and said you didn't want to be a hassle on our big day. I finally said, "We have six months to talk about it." Little did I know that was going to be the last day I would ever see you. I remember you were almost in tears that day, mainly because you cared for Jeanette so much. Finally, after three and a half years I finally asked her to marry me, and you couldn't have been more happy for us. We laughed and talked some more, and as I drove away, you smiled. I remember shouting out the car window as we drove away, "First row, Marie! August 29th!"

This was right around the time I was involved in a junior high group, and all my junior highers loved Marie almost as much as I did. The Sunday after Jeanette and I had sprung the news, one of my junior high kids came up to me before I started the service and told me he'd seen Marie's wheelchair on the side of the road today, but that she wasn't in it, just a bunch of flowers.

I will never forget February 1, 1998—the day I saw your empty

wheelchair on Chapman Boulevard. I knew instantly something
was different—probably because you weren't in it. You had
left this place. Your wheelchair was still there, but no one was
smiling and no one was waving. I learned that you had suffered
another stroke and passed away in the middle of the night. I
couldn't believe what I was hearing and broke down right in the
front office. I walked out to the side of the road where your chair
was and noticed the flowers and pictures that covered your chair.
As I headed into your room, I knew you left something for me.
I cried walking into your room, but I started to smile when I
opened up that drawer and found six bananas waiting for me.

I knew how much Marie meant to me, but I didn't know how much her
simple act of waving meant to so many people. The retirement home
left her wheelchair on the side of the road for a week, and after just
those seven days, it was completely obscured by all the flowers, letters,
balloons, and other items people from the town had brought. I visited
the chair several times that week and watched people come by to drop
off things and engage in this moment. As I watched these people stop by,
I realized how much they'd missed by not really knowing Marie. If only
they would have stopped their cars a week or a year earlier—that's when
Marie really needed them, but most of them were all too busy to take a
minute out of their busy schedules and spend it with this great lady.

I was fortunate enough to meet Marie, and at the time of her passing she
was closer to me than any of my own family members. I wanted others
to know Marie and wished I could share some of her stories with them,
so with the help of the local paper, I organized a memorial service to be
held at the church where I worked. I had no idea who would come out to
a service for a lady only a few people actually knew, but I was determined
and went through with it anyway.

I cancelled the junior high group meeting that night and had all my junior high students present at the memorial service in the hopes they would pad the attendance a little. Boy, was I wrong. By 7:00 p.m., there were a few hundred people seated in the auditorium. The service began with local singer/songwriter Jacob Vanauken performing a song he'd written about Marie, and then I got up to speak. I read a letter to the audience that I'd written shortly after I heard the news of her passing (you just finished reading some of it). We were friends for three years, and oh, how she blessed my life! I am such a better person and friend to others because of the things Marie showed me. As I shared and the people listened, there were some tears and some laughter, but the overall feeling I got from the audience was, "Man, we really missed our chance, and we can't get it back."

I know I almost missed my chance. That first day I got out of the car to talk to her wasn't the first day I'd seen her. I'd noticed her for months before I ever did anything about it, before I decided I needed to do something. I needed a story; I needed an experience of my own. The Scriptures are powerful and should challenge people to move out of their comfort zones and into the realm of action.

So often pastors or professional speakers can say all the right things and have three-point sermons that sound great, but the Bible should compel you past words and into action. Jesus' words are not meant just to be read once a week, or heard on Sunday morning. Jesus spent little time actually speaking; He was mostly involved in doing. The Bible says, "Faith without works is dead" (James 2:26). I am not saying that you can earn your salvation through works, but without works, there is no proof of your commitment. Christianity is supposed to be lived out in your life twenty-four hours a day, seven days a week, 365 days a year.

The day I met Marie, I drove down Chapman Boulevard like every other day, but as I honked and waved at her, I knew I had to do more. I did not hear a voice from God telling me to stop my car; I just knew waving and honking wasn't going to cut it. She needed far more than a loud noise;

she needed a relationship. I realized that day that Jesus was probably not going to use my horn or my hand to bring Marie to Him, but He could use me. My first step that day was getting out of my car, shutting the door, and walking over to meet the lady who would one day refer to me as "her boy."

I easily could have missed the opportunity God gave me that day to make a difference. I realized I needed some sort of movement in my Christian faith, but I didn't expect what happened when I took action—I didn't expect to receive the biggest blessing imaginable. That day, God connected me with a woman who became closer than a family member, a friend I never would have expected.

When we go to the gutter, we aren't just changing gutter-dwellers; they're changing us. We're all being changed for the better. Too often we sit through church, and when it's over, we think we're done with our work for the week. That is wrong, wrong, wrong. You cannot live out your faith based solely on what other people tell you; you cannot be okay with merely consuming information—including the information in this book. You must be convicted to take action for God.

You may not be a youth pastor at a youth conference, but what if you're a businessman at a convention? You may not be a lovable but gruff senior citizen on a street corner, but what if you're a high school student in the lunchroom? The point of our Christian lives is to take Christ with us everywhere we go, all the time, no matter what. It's about beating back the frustration, the aggravation, and the outright attacks from the enemy and letting our light shine in a dark place. It's about taking what God has given us—whether it's a corner of the street or a captive audience of 70,000 people—and using it. It's about putting Christ's love into action.

Marie took action, and it was just a simple wave. I took action, and it was just a simple push of the brake pedal. Action isn't complicated, but it can have a powerful *re*action that lasts and lasts.

# CHAPTER TWELVE

Oh, one last thing about Marie. The spot where she planted her wheelchair every day? It was right above a gutter.

She affected a city with a simple wave of her hand. Imagine what you can do. Go.

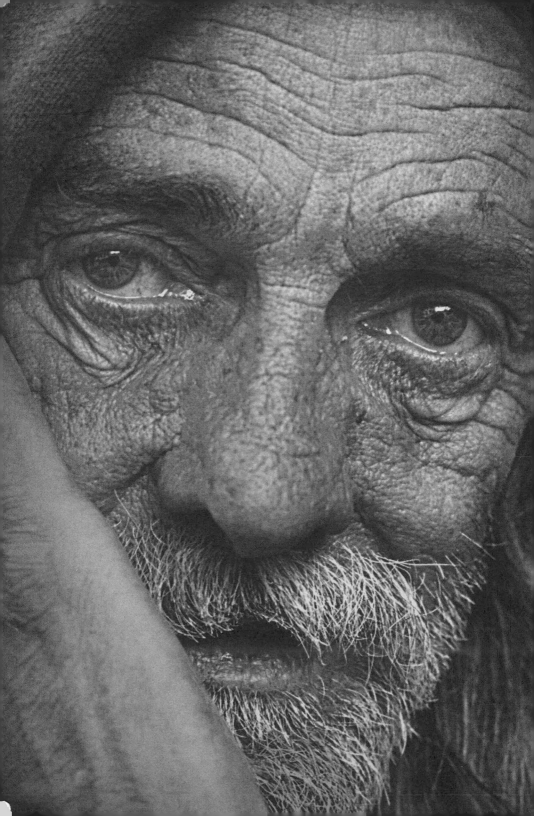

# HAVE YOU GONE?
## THINKING ABOUT GOING?

( Looking for a little encouragement? )

## YOUR STORY CONTINUES AT
*www.getinthegutter.com.*

# [RELEVANTBOOKS]